CW00921207

Dealing with Difficult People
secrets

The experts tell all!

About the author
David Brown MCIPD studied mechanical engineering at Loughborough University and secured a diploma in Management Studies from the University of Aston. For the last 20 years he has been a consultant and coach specializing in improving business performance.

Author's note
David has a diploma in Neuro Linguistic Programming (NLP), which offers an insight into behaviours and relationship building. For more information visit www.scott-brown.co.uk. David wishes to acknowledge the considerable contribution made by his associate, Norman Leet, in the writing of this book.

Dealing with
Difficult People
secrets

Collins
A division of HarperCollins*Publishers*
77-85 Fulham Palace Road, London W6 8JB

www.BusinessSecrets.net

First published in Great Britain in 2010 by HarperCollins*Publishers*
Published in Canada by HarperCollins*Canada*. www.harpercollins.ca
Published in Australia by HarperCollins*Australia*. www.harpercollins.com.au
Published in India by HarperCollins*PublishersIndia*. www.harpercollins.co.in

1

A catalogue record for this book is available from the British Library.

ISBN 978-0-00-734677-6

Printed and bound at Clays Ltd, St Ives plc

Contents

Work successfully with difficult people

If someone is being difficult in a business situation, the end result is that individuals, teams or the organization as a whole will find it difficult to function effectively and be as successful as they otherwise might. This book gives you the skills to address difficult people and difficult situations.

I have been in many situations where someone has been widely considered 'difficult'. It can make life frustrating and even deeply unpleasant. Whilst this book will offer you lots of tips about how to handle such people, we will also look a little deeper at what makes people difficult. You will be asked also to consider situations in which you might be the cause of difficult behaviour – I know that I have sometimes been considered to be the difficult one, when I was quite sure that others were being difficult!

Once you understand the root of the difficulty, you can work out a remedial strategy to suit the situation. This book captures 50 **secrets** presented in seven chapters that provide the key to you dealing with difficult people. You need to decide which tip will help you in which situation.

■ **Understand what makes us tick.** If you are to manage difficult behaviour successfully, you need to understand behaviour! Consider what shapes our behaviour, what behaviours you can realistically expect to change – and what you can't.

■ **Look in the mirror.** You may be the problem. This chapter helps you to understand yourself and to consider how you appear to others.

■ **Step into their shoes.** If you are to help people see the need for change, you need to understand those people and discover why they are different to you. In this chapter you will be offered tips on how to create trust and rapport before attempting change.

■ **Give difficult people a chance.** There is a need for you to display leadership, even though sometimes you may not be the line manager. We will look at clear outcomes, role clarity, reinforcing appropriate behaviour and helpful communication.

■ **Use the right tool for the situation.** There are many tools that can help you manage difficult behaviour and difficult situations. Here are some of the globally accepted tools, including some psychometrics, with tips on when to use them.

■ **Develop your skills.** This chapter draws on the previous Secrets to develop your all-round ability to deal with difficult people.

■ **Resolve conflicts effectively.** We conclude with a series of checklists which will help you decide how to move forward with your 'difficult person'.

If you find yourself saying, "that person is difficult", don't condemn them before you have exhausted all the possible strategies for dealing with difficult people covered in these **secrets**. You may not be able to change their personality, but you can change their behaviour.

Use these secrets to promote harmony and deliver results.

Understand what makes us tick

People that we label 'difficult' appear so because they behave differently to us – in a manner that we may even deem unacceptable. If we are to deal successfully with difficult behaviour, we need to understand some of the fundamentals of human behaviour. This chapter offers an understanding of how we are all different, and why these differences exist. We will look at assertiveness, different communication styles, and how we all see the world through individual eyes.

1.1

Define what you mean by difficult

When problem-solving you need first to define the problem and then form a clear view of what a good solution, or outcome, will look like. If we are to manage difficult people successfully, we need to be clear about what we mean by the term 'difficult'.

People don't normally turn up for work determined to be difficult. People that you find 'difficult' are only difficult because they are different to you, or disagree with you, or behave in a fashion that you or your colleagues find unacceptable. Being difficult takes many forms and is a matter of perception. You will have your own criteria for what makes people difficult, but here are a few examples:

case study I worked for five years with someone who was forever pushing, shaping and driving his own agenda. He constantly interrupted colleagues in mid-sentence. Everyone who worked with him thought him difficult, but he was a significant factor in our team's success. My feedback, aimed at changing his behaviour,

■ **Perfectionists.** If you want a quick result, perfectionists can be infuriating. If you are the perfectionist, you will irritate those who think that good enough is okay and makes economic sense.

■ **Control freaks.** These types will annoy you by interfering when you want to be left alone to do things your way.

■ **Creative people.** They are a must if ideas are an essential part of moving forward but can be painful when you just want to get on with delivering a simple result.

■ **Shapers.** They drive the action (see Secret 5.8) and are vital in a successful team, but they take over as and when they see fit.

■ **Aggressive or defensive people.** Few people welcome aggression in business. People who are always on the defensive present problems as well. We need assertive people (see Secret 1.5).

■ **Submissive people.** This kind of behaviour can be caused by many things, including childhood experiences and feeling threatened. Their lack of confidence and fear of failure can be frustrating.

The examples above are caused by a host of different things, and that makes all of us different. Potentially, that makes all of us difficult in some people's eyes. We need to understand enough about ourselves and others to recognize what we can reasonably expect to change and what we should find a way of living with.

Understand that everyone behaves differently to you.

had no effect whatsoever. One day we did a Belbin analysis (Secret 5.8) and he registered the most extreme shaper score that I have ever seen. I then concluded that this was so much a part of his personality that we needed to move him out of our team or accept him for what he was. We chose to live with him.

1.2

Accept that we are all different

'Difficult' might just mean 'different'. This Secret will help you understand different people, so that you can accept some differences before deciding what is unacceptable and needs changing. So what causes all of us to be different?

■ **Values.** You may value punctuality but have a colleague who considers that any time will do. Many organizations promote key values to engender harmony, but an individualist may struggle to accept them.

■ **Beliefs.** Different political, cultural and religious beliefs can limit our ability to work with others.

■ **Gender.** Although some women are more aggressive than some men, on the whole women are inclined to be more empathetic than men, to value security more and to put greater emphasis on teamwork.

> **case study** Recently I managed a project where one member of the team would say things like, "that could backfire on you" or "that won't work". Her glass was 'half empty', as it were. Another team member would regularly say, "it's worth a try". There was no right or

■ **Personality.** Our personalities are a complex web of background, culture, beliefs, values, genes and more besides. Some combine well and productively, some abrasively yet still productively, while others are unmitigated disasters. We need to accept, though, that mankind thrives because of our differences – we need to use difference, not stifle it.

Before leaving the question of differences, consider NLP (Neuro Linguistic Programming) filters. We all see the world through different filters, and if you understand this you will be well placed to manage the differences through better communication. Our different filters include:

■ **Internal/external.** If you ask an 'internal' person, "How will you know you have succeeded?", they will say, "I'll just know". Whereas the 'external' person will say, "I'll know from the feedback I get".
■ **Towards/away from.** A 'towards' person will take risks. An 'away' person will see problems.
■ **Same/difference.** A 'same' person will refer to what they've always done: "it's like I did last month". Whereas the 'difference' person will say, "let's try a new approach". The latter will need variety; the former may be reluctant to change.
■ **Problems/solutions.** Some people always see the problem, while others focus on the solution.

Welcome the differences around you, and only see them as a problem when they are a barrier to results.

wrong – just healthy differences that were part of a successful project. If you want to get the best from a 'half empty' person, you need to match their language and make references to 'half empty' things, even if you are inclined to be 'half full' yourself.

1.3

Ensure communication is two-way

One-way communication is a closed system. It is limiting and leads to frustration. This Secret explains how to ensure that communication is two-way, constructive and likely to promote good relationships.

When I was struggling to understand why someone failed to respond to one of my memos, one of my colleagues said, "David, it's no good you being pleased with your communication. Your message is only okay if it produces the results that you require." He went on to explain that the recipient's perception of the message is every bit as important as your message. It has to be a two-way thing. Here are a few suggestions that will help you to be on the same wavelength as someone with whom you are working.

case study Here's a lesson I learnt about always making sure that your language is correctly understood by all concerned. As a young man I went on a course where we played management games. One involved creating patterns from dominoes. We

■ **Accept that their perception is reality to them.** The challenge is to understand them and their situation well enough to find common ground. This means taking time to understand the belief systems and values that others hold.

■ **Know yourself.** You need to be clear about your own beliefs, and when they might prevent you from taking on board a good idea. There is a constant need to be open-minded to fresh ideas.

■ **Be aware of other ways of thinking.** There are plenty of other filters besides those mentioned in the last Secret; some people talk detail, others look at the big picture; some like choices and some like a rigid system; some people are mainly reactive and others proactive. To increase rapport you should be prepared to enter another person's world. If you are a strategic thinker, for example, take time to explore detail with those who relish the minutiae.

■ **Talk their language, paint them a picture.** Appreciate that, if someone prefers to visualize rather than verbalize, you'll need to use language that they might use, such as, "This is what it will look like."

■ **Mutual respect.** Above all, you need to respect each other before you can hope to work effectively together. You don't need to like each other, but you do need to establish a basis of mutual respect before difficult transactions.

Keep asking: are you on the same wavelength as others?

debated what to do with a 'three four' and a 'double six'. It took 30 minutes before one of our team asked the question, "What's a double six?" He was Korean, and none of us had bothered to think about his culture or to check his understanding of our language!

1.4

Manage change

Unless they are helping to shape it, people usually resist change. Sometimes this is because they resent a new situation being 'sold' to them, and sometimes it is because of what they think they will lose or leave behind. Good management can ease the transition.

When helping organizations manage change, I seek to show people that change is inevitable because of the way that the world around us is changing – standing still is not an option. Changes around any business demand changes within that business for it to survive.

With individuals, though, it is difficult for most of us to change our behaviour – even when we want to in order to lose weight, for example, or give up smoking. Most of us have an inbuilt resistance to change, and, in busines, this often results in a serious drop in performance. This is summed up in a well-known model called the Change Curve. However, this dip in performance and the duration of the 'curve' can be lessened through good management. Remember, change is not

case study I was involved in a takeover that resulted in strike action before the two companies joined forces. Staff in one of the businesses were afraid of the merger because their business had been performing badly.

"Change is the only certainty in life"

Henry A. Wallace, US Vice President 1941-5

only about where people are going: it's what people think they are losing that leads to the most resistance. So to manage transition successfully, you and your organization should do the following:

■ **Share your vision.** Communicate on a regular basis about where you are going and why. Start with the end in mind.

■ **Respect the past.** Don't expect people to leap from the present straight to your version of the future. Check that people understand what is being asked of them; that they are ready to move; that they are capable of making the change; that progress can be monitored and the right support given.

■ **Consult people.** Involve them in what you seek to do.

■ **Show people what's in it for them.** Appeal to their emotions as much as their logic.

■ **Check for 'buy in'.** Where are people on the Change Curve? Seek out negative feelings behind any negative action.

■ **Pull together.** Agree realistic SMART targets (see Secret 5.3).

■ **The Six 'R's.** Reinforce, reinforce, reinforce. Review, review, review.

If you are to bring about successful change, study the change process.

They were, in fact, highly regarded by the incoming management team, but were unaware of this as insufficient information had been shared with them. The steps outlined above would have avoided the problem.

1.5

Understand assertiveness

Behaving assertively is crucial for good interpersonal relationships. We need to understand the term, though, in respect of three contrasting types of behaviour: aggressive, passive and assertive.

1 **Aggressive behaviour (I win/you lose).** Driven by a self-centred attitude, whereby their needs and rights are always paramount. Outward signs include a harsh, loud voice, interrupting others and aggressive body language. It could be caused by fear, insecurity or ambition. Aggressive people may get what they want in the short term, but in the long run alienate themselves and are often rejected as too difficult.

2 **Passive behaviour (I lose/you win).** Driven by a sense that their rights and needs are less important than other people's. Outward signs include quietness, hesitancy and nervous body movements. Shyness, a lack of confidence or ambition, or a strong sense of team can prompt this. They may get what they want by manipulating those around them (they get others to do the tricky bits), but in the short term do not seem to achieve.

3 **Assertive behaviour (I win/you win).** Assertive behaviour is what you need to get results through people. Difficult people melt away if your approach is, "I recognize that you have needs and rights. I too have needs. I respect you, and I require reciprocal respect from you."

A balanced individual will display assertive behaviour most of the time. To avoid slipping into passive or aggressive behaviour:

■ **Define your goals.** Decide where you are going.
■ **Help others to express their views.** Question their thinking.
■ **Listen to others.** Check what you've heard them say to make sure your understanding is correct before you respond.
■ **Have a clear contract with them.** This is about give and take and mutual respect (this won't necessarily mean 50/50 with your boss!).
■ **Share feelings.** Have both of you share your feelings with one another as well as the facts.
■ **Spell out clearly what you mean.** Be straightforward. Explain the consequences of their action.
■ **Say no when you must, and explain why.** If remedial action is called for, do it sooner rather than later. Sooner is easier!
■ **Accept that other people have a right to say no.** Understand why they are saying no. This could be a deep-rooted cultural question.
■ **Be positive.** Use positive words and body language (Secret 6.4).

Be assertive yourself and encourage the same behaviour in others.

1.6

Find the causes of discord

It is very easy to make superficial judgements about what to do with difficult people. But this can cause us to miss the root cause of the discord. Look at the details and consider each case individually.

Difficult people will take up a disproportionate amount of your time, so it is in your interests to invest time to get to the bottom of why they behave as they do. Suppose you feel that someone is a bully. You could try facing up to them, because, when confronted, bullies often do back down. That's the superficial approach, though, and the case study below invites you to look under the skin of the difficult person before deciding on your strategy for dealing with them.

case study You need to be aware that someone could be difficult because of physical or mental health problems. It's not your job to solve their problems, but it is your responsibility to be on the lookout for such contributory factors. An MD asked me to help design a performance management system. One of the issues that surfaced was that the Sales Director was seen to

Language discord

Another approach to understanding discord involves realizing that we have preferences regarding our thought processes and language. There are three different ways in which we show our language preferences:

■ **Visual.** The visual type will say, "I see what you mean", "Let's look at this one more time" or "It's quite clear to me".
■ **Audio.** The audio type will say, "Let's talk about it", "I'm speechless" or "Go and shout this from the rooftops".
■ **Kinesthetic.** This person is all about feeling. "I feel this is wrong for us", "She's a very warm-hearted person" or "I sense you don't like this".

The problem is that if you prefer one of these three, and the person in front of you prefers others, then you will have discord and a potentially difficult person. The answer is (a) for you to use a balanced blend of these styles, and (b) to match your style to those around you, where possible. So, if someone is regularly using kinesthetic/feeling words, use such words yourself.

Look what's behind the behaviour before you decide how to respond

bully two of his staff with sustained and systematic ridicule. We explained the impact that he was having, and we faced the problem head on by warning the bully of the consequences of his actions. We did things by the book, but only by digging deeper did we discover that he was an alcoholic. We enlisted specialist help, and the problem was controlled.

Look in the mirror

Very few people are difficult. They only seem so when they interact with other people, including you! Through the Secrets in this chapter, you will be introduced to the concept of emotional intelligence, you will gain a better understanding of yourself and you'll be asked to consider how you appear to others. This will give you the best possible chance of working successfully with those around you — even with the people who seem truly difficult.

2.1

Develop your emotional intelligence

Emotional intelligence (EI) is the capacity to recognize our own feelings and those of others, and to manage our own emotions and the emotions of others with whom we have relationships. We are born with EI, but it can be developed further.

There are five core emotions – fear, anger, sadness, joy and disgust. Emotions are usually at the root of difficult behaviour, and you are likely to meet them with an emotional reaction yourself. If you are emotionally intelligent, though, you will manage your own emotions and take into account other people's needs and concerns.

case study The MD of a fork-lift truck distributor had a management team of five. He was autocratic, aggressive and obstinate, yet also direct, organized and financially astute. Sadly, he never learned from his experiences because he had a fixed view of his own capability and how his team should be handled. He always behaved the same way and he always got the

Here are five key points to help develop your emotional intelligence:

■ **Be self aware.** Know your values, ambitions, preferences, intuitions and confidence levels. Know how you will respond to pressure.
■ **Regulate yourself.** Manage your disruptive emotions, maintain your standards of integrity, be flexible in handling change, take responsibility for your performance and be comfortable with new ideas.
■ **Manage your motivation.** Align yourself with the goals of your team and organization; overcome obstacles to your goals.
■ **Display empathy.** Be sensitive to other people's feelings. Recognize the need for diverse talents. Be aware of the emotional tide within a group, and understand where the power lies. Know how others perceive you.
■ **Have social skills.** Use the right tactics to persuade; agree collective goals; listen before you lead. Inspire others with your judgement, communication, collaboration and management of change. Provide feedback to suit the situation.

This is a taste of EI, and a formidable list of competencies. Why is this important to you as you deal with difficult people? Quite simply, if emotions such as anxiety and anger are not addressed in your quest for performance, you and those around you will not perform well.

How well do you manage your own emotions and the emotions of others?

same results – including a frustrated team that could not stand up to him. He nagged them rather than coached them. He didn't develop, his frustrated people didn't grow and the business had to be rescued. If he had developed his emotional intelligence and adapted his behaviour to suit each situation, he would have discovered that 'soft' skills deliver 'hard' results.

2.2

Understand your own reactions

You are an important part of any situation involving difficult people, so you need to understand yourself and your reaction to difficult situations. Armed with self-knowledge, you can avoid the mistake of putting people in pigeon holes and, instead, treat each situation individually.

Let's explore why you react as you do. What might cause you to lose control of your emotions? It might happen when:

■ You feel that your fundamental beliefs or values are threatened.
■ You sense you are being treated unfairly.
■ Someone lets you or your team down.
■ You are overloaded.
■ Your intentions are misunderstood or misinterpreted.
■ You make an embarrassing mistake.
■ Others lose their temper.
■ You are cornered, with no choice or options.
■ Your ambitions or goals are threatened.
■ You are irritated by a personal emotional trigger.

"Emotional strength comes from self discovery and self mastery"

Bossidy and Charan, authors of Execution

The secret is to develop your skill at handling yourself before you engage with others, as it's important to respond in a calm way rather than adding to the emotional cocktail of a difficult situation. If you don't, *you* are likely to be the 'difficult one'.

■ **Know yourself.** Be aware of how you react and what causes you to lose control of your emotions. Are you confused, embarrassed, frightened, disgusted, angry or sad? You need to ask yourself about what you feel and why you feel as you do before you can handle difficult people.

■ **Listen to others.** Listening to others and acknowledging how they feel will defuse the emotions that make life difficult, and give you time to understand yourself and them. Accept that listening takes time.

■ **Stay calm**. Develop relaxation techniques. Take a few deep breaths.

■ **React to what's around you.** You need to take note of the system in which you operate. Allow for company procedures, the law and the interests of others in the company. This requires objectivity, detachment and structure.

■ **Respond to the person.** It is important to attend to the needs and feelings of others. This requires that you understand the truth as perceived by them. We'll look at this more thoroughly in Chapter 3.

Know yourself if you are to work successfully with others.

2.3

Check your confidence levels

'Confidence' comes from the Latin *confidere*, which means to trust. If you are to handle difficult people, they need to trust you, which means that you have to trust yourself. You need to trust your motives, your decision making and your people skills.

Confidence goes hand in hand with assertiveness, which is distinct from aggression or over-confidence (see Secret 1.5) It's other people's perceptions of you that matter here, but there are steps you can take to ensure that your confidence is at an appropriate level. You should first ask yourself a few questions:

■ When do you feel comfortable, and when do you feel out of your comfort zone?
■ How comfortable are you with what you have achieved in life?
■ Where do you add value, and where do you add little value?
■ How well equipped are you to do your job?
■ When might you need to be more decisive or inclined to take risks?
■ When do nerves inhibit your performance? When does your body language betray you?
■ When do you ever feel the need to cover up a lack of confidence?

"People become what they believe themselves to be. If I believe I can do things I acquire the ability to do it." Mahatma Ghandi

■ Do you harbour any self-limiting beliefs about yourself? Do you contribute as fully as you should?
■ Do you feel in control of your life at work?
■ Are you overly concerned about what people think of you?

Reflect on your answers to the questions. They can be connected with many things – meeting the 'big boss' for the first time, speaking to 30 people, an unpleasant experience or a lack of key skills. The trick is to look for clues and patterns, and then do something about it:

■ **Remind yourself of your successes.** What are you good at?
■ **Treat yourself.** Maximize your time spent with people who appreciate you and in situations in which you excel.
■ **Address your development needs.** Share your ideas with a trusted colleague. Consider training, coaching or mentoring.
■ **Visualize being successful.** Top sportspeople do this; it breeds success!
■ **Open an achievement bank.** Create a log of your successes.
■ **Learn from your mistakes.** But don't be inhibited by them.
■ **Set achievable goals.** Recognize that you can't be good at everything.

In short - take stock of yourself; know what you are capable of; keep learning; be prepared to develop your capability by stepping outside your comfort zone and live with ambiguity.

For others to have confidence in you, develop your own confidence.

2.4

Ask yourself, "How do I look to others?"

If only we could be as honest with ourselves as we are with other people, we would see ourselves as others do. Then, armed with an accurate perception of how others see us, we would be better able to get on their wavelength and bridge the gaps between us.

Everyone sees you differently, but it is helpful if your perception and theirs line up. Consider a set of personal qualities that are important, such as those listed in the chart, opposite. Rate how people see you on a scale of 0 to 10 (the numbers don't imply any relative merit, such as good and bad, only difference).

Have a conversation with someone about how they see you, and reciprocate by offering your view of them. Start with someone you trust, before moving on to someone with whom you have problems. Ask for specific examples that support their views of you. The result should be a constructive, honest sharing of perceptions that leads to development needs that can be worked on. You will get to know each other better, and should find each other less difficult.

If you do this exercise with an entire team, make team player/ individual one of the criteria.

> "It is difficult to be honest with yourself. It is much easier to be honest with other people."

Edward Benson (1867- 1940), English author

Characteristics to be rated		How others see you
Rated 0	Rated 10	Rating (0–10)
Extrovert	Introvert	
Circumspect	Straightforward	
Emotional	Logical	
Indifferent	Enthusiastic	
Nervous	Confident	
Passive	Controlling	
Conventional	Creative	
Trusting	Suspicious	
Uncaring	Caring	
Closed	Open	

I have used this tool to good effect to sort out differences with regard to confused priorities, different values, fears, low self-esteem, plus a lack of transparency and openness.

Whether you use it one-on-one or within a team, whether you record the results or just have a chat, this tool is a way of checking how your personal 'brand' is being received within your organization. If properly used in conjunction with the tools in Chapter 5, it can become an even more powerful remedy for removing barriers and promoting harmony in your place of work.

To understand yourself better, ask how others perceive you.

Step into their shoes

If you are finding a relationship difficult, the 'chemistry' is not quite right. We have looked at your part of the chemistry in the last chapter. Now it's time to look at the other party, and step into their shoes. Only by understanding their perspective will you appreciate what you need to do to help them change their behaviour. Then the relationship will be more enjoyable and more productive.

3.1

First take off your own shoes

If you see everything through your own eyes, you will never understand other people's points of view. This Secret will help you relate to others and learn how to influence them.

Difficult people are unlikely to see themselves as the problem, so you need to go out of your way to understand them. Then, armed with knowledge, you can decide on your strategy for changing the nature of your relationship. Here are a few things to consider:

■ **Don't rush.** Take time to react, to understand the other person's wants and needs, the system in which you are operating and the context. Don't make this an interrogation; have a conversation.

case study Roda and I worked on a project that involved government funding. Roda wanted marketing support, and quickly. She felt that her company had a decent business plan, and that she was close to being the complete manager. I felt that she had no perception of what marketing meant, had a mishmash of

"If you are to step into someone else's shoes then first you must take off your own" Mark Twain, American author

■ **Respond.** Personalize your approach to them.

■ **Create a dialogue.** Invite emotions to be revealed, because behaviour is only the tip of the iceberg – what lies under the surface are beliefs, attitudes and motivation that you need to understand.

■ **Spot the emotions.** Emotions drive behaviour. Try to pick up on feelings of hurt, fear, anger, sadness, shock, frustration, confusion, etc.

■ **Dissipate anger.** Let them talk anger out of their system.

■ **Listen actively.** Understand what's behind the words you hear.

■ **Check their style.** Ask yourself whether their preferred style is audio, visual or kinesthetic (see Secret 1.6). Match their preference. Watch for a clue in their eye movements: visual people will tend to look up; audio people to the side; kinesthetic types tend to cast their eyes down.

■ **Replay and check.** Explain back to them what you understand them to be saying. Check that you are both on the same wavelength.

Before you can influence others, first see the world from their perspective.

documents that was nothing like a business plan, and she would have been considered by most people to be difficult. Our relationship struggled. With hindsight, in the early stages I should have put myself in her shoes more than I did, and delivered more of what she wanted before addressing my own agenda.

3.2

Be specific

If you are to reach an understanding of how another person thinks, you need to avoid generalizations and identify how you see them in specific terms. To label someone 'aggressive', for example, is unhelpful and may make a problem worse. Whereas being specific will help you decide what to do in any situation.

Saying to Linda, "your attitude to Mary is all wrong" will antagonize her. If, on the other hand, you say, "I want you to take the trouble to understand Mary's situation, particularly why it is that she can't start work till 9.30am," then she knows what you want. This Secret is about forming a specific view in your head before you engage your mouth, so that you can manage the situation better.

To clarify your thoughts on someone, understand what they seek to achieve in their job, and then consider the qualities that they need to succeed in that job. I like to break these down into **Attitudes**, **Skills** and **Knowledge**. A few examples for a buyer might be:

case study I was recently asked to observe and facilitate a faltering relationship. Both parties agreed to a psychometric test (see Secret 5.10) which helped us see aspects of the two people that were not clear to

■ **Attitudes.** Seeks good relationships with other departments and with suppliers. Is profit-conscious.

■ **Skills.** Negotiates profitably. Uses time effectively.

■ **Knowledge.** Knows our internal systems. Knows our requirements.

For each of these attributes, form a specific view of the buyer. Can you justify to yourself the view that you have of them? Did they demonstrate good use of their time? This is effectively a performance review process to form a clear view of the problem you have to solve.

Another way of identifying a problem is to involve a third party to help you with a three-way discussion. What you discuss depends upon the situation, but it could include:

■ How do you see the situation?
■ What exactly has happened?
■ What were the consequences; what makes it a problem?
■ How does this affect the results of your work?
■ How do you feel about it?
■ What are your expectations in this respect?
■ What would be a satisfactory outcome?

Putting people in boxes is unhelpful. Take a fresh look at each person in each situation in order to develop your skills and give yourself choices with regard to how you handle people.

Form a clear, specific view of the difficult person before tackling the problem.

them. One was strong on emotion, the other preferred logic. Once they understood and accepted the differences between them that the test had highlighted, they were able to work together more constructively.

3.3

Ask yourself how they are different to you

In the last Secret we pinpointed a problem. Now I will ask you to define the differences that you have identified before we move on to address them.

If you can understand the nature of personal differences, you will be better placed to bridge the gap between you. So what should you look for? Here are six key differences:

1 Is one of you quick and impatient; the other patient and slow?
2 Does one of you seek to control everything and everybody, while the other leaves people to get on with things?
3 Is one of you a perfectionist; the other more relaxed about quality?
4 Is one of you assertive (presumably you!); the other aggressive?

case study I was working with a team leader who had difficulties engaging with his staff. They thought him to be a closed book, and very clinical. I asked him, "Where would you put yourself on the emotional/rational scale?" He said, "Almost 100% inclined to start with feelings and emotion." I asked, "Then why have we just

5 Is one consultative or collaborative; the other dictatorial?
6 Is one of you people-centred; the other driven by the task?

These are all differences that are readily apparent. As with us all, you will have labels put on you that sum up your style – the general way you do things. What should you do about this?

■ **Accept differences.** All styles have their uses and strengths.
■ **Respect others.** Don't expect everybody to be the same as you.
■ **Decide.** As well as deciding what you will tolerate, decide what differ-ences are unacceptable/detrimental to you or the organization.
■ **Differentiate.** Separate those things that you can realistically change from those things that you can't. Form a view of how realistic it is for someone to let go of a specific behaviour and embrace another.
■ **Talk about it.** People are often unaware of how others see them or even how they see themselves. The answer is to talk about it.

Ask yourself how people are different to you before you try to change things.

spent 10 minutes talking about a problem person, focusing on nothing but targets and data?" "I got that wrong, didn't I?" he said quickly! Asking him to rate himself revealed more to him than I ever could by telling him. He went on to accept that he should take more time to understand the hopes and fears of his team.

3.4

Accept some differences

Sometimes you have to accept differences simply because some factors in a situation cannot be changed. You must draw a distinction between things you can change and things you can't.

The differences in style referred to in the previous Secret stem from differences in personality. Some of these are very deep-seated and you will never change them. It could be a lot easier to find the person in question another job in the company, or even another company if the personality issue is serious enough!

Some situations that might be too difficult to change

■ If two people have a deep-seated dislike of each other, it may be more realistic and effective to find ways for them to work through other people, rather than expect them to work together harmoniously.

> **case study** When I worked as a young sales manager, we had a customer who simply could not get on with our account manager. There was nothing wrong with either of them — they were both extremely personable

"Never try to teach a pig to sing; it wastes your time and annoys the pig" Paul Dickson, American author

■ Your boss may be poor at absorbing detail when you brief him or her. If so, be judicious about how much detail you give in one go.

■ Some technicians and software designers lack people skills. Be prepared to accept that you might have to work round the interpersonal problems to benefit from a great technician.

■ It is unlikely that you'll persuade an introvert to become an extrovert. You may change them slightly, but don't be over-ambitious.

When can we expect people to change?

■ If people are hostile because they are fearful of others, or fear for their jobs, then, providing we understand the fear and tackle the root cause, we have a right to ask them to modify their behaviour.

■ If someone feels powerless and fails to engage in the business, the same applies. Help them understand how they make a difference. Then you can expect them to get more involved.

■ If someone lacks confidence in their ability to do their job, then they may need to be trained or coached. Only then can you reasonably expect them to display confidence.

Make sound judgements about how much people are capable of changing.

— but the chemistry between them was awful. I quickly decided not to invest time striving to understand the chemistry and bring them together. We changed the account manager, and just put it down to experience.

3.5

Focus on what motivates

To influence someone who is presenting you with difficulties, you need to understand what motivates them. Find what will motivate them to change, and you will be well on the way to realizing that change.

There is a link between values (what's important to us), beliefs (what's right and wrong) and personality. All these things have a part to play in what motivates us, what we seek to achieve, and how we go about it (our behaviour).

People may be motivated by status, promotion, power, belonging, shared values, praise, feeling useful, risk, security, pay and many other things. Studies show that money is not a long-term motivator, but that poor reward can be a de-motivator.

case study I ran a series of performance management workshops for a chain of private hospitals in the UK. We were looking at motivation levels with a view to improve performance. One manager said to his team, "As long as I am the manager, performance reviews will be linked to pay." At another hospital, a different

The symptoms of poor motivation – conflict, apathy, absenteeism, resistance to change, etc – are often associated with difficult people. Successful people understand what motivates others, and they make conscious or subconscious appeals to people who they seek to influence. You can do this in several ways:

■ **Use empathy.** The emotionally intelligent will simply read people intuitively to get the best out of them. They don't have to try too hard.
■ **Read the books.** There is much material to help you understand motivation (see further reading). Fundamentally, though, you must decide whether you believe people need motivating (by you or others) or whether, in a reasonable environment, they will motivate themselves. I subscribe to the latter view.
■ **Focus on the individual.** What drives a difficult person? This is a big part of your difficulty. What might persuade them to change what they do? There has to be something in it for them!
■ **Think about the timeline.** Think in terms of where they've come from, where they are and where they want to go – their ambition. Is there a lack of alignment between where you are asking them to go and where they want to go? If, for instance, there are limited opportunities for promotion and the person seeks career advancement, you need to find compensating factors that will make up for lack of advancement.

If you want people to change, appeal to what turns them on.

manager said, "It is unrealistic to expect someone to discuss personal development if they know it will affect their pay. We must separate performance and pay reviews by six months." Both views can be justified, but each has to cater for different assumptions about to what degree money is a motivating factor.

3.6

Establish trust

If you seek to change people before they are ready, you will fail. We touched on this in Secret 1.4. Now let's help you develop a relationship that is based on the other person trusting you before you attempt to change them or what is around them. What is the key to someone trusting you?

■ **People need to know that you are on their side.** Demonstrate that you are in tune with them and their needs. You don't have to agree with them, but you do have to understand what is important to them.

■ **They need to feel that you understand their situation.** A part of this involves you showing that it is okay for them to be different.

■ **Resist the temptation to fix 'them'.** If you let people assume control over their feelings, their emotions and their actions, they will be more motivated to embrace change than if you push them.

■ **Recognize their problems.** They may be to do with work relationships; a lack of confidence or skill; or even personal matters. It may not

case study When asked to help two people who were at loggerheads, I asked them to use the 'two boxes' approach. They each summarized their view and the view of the other person, as they saw it. The boxes

be your place to solve their personal problems, but you need to allow for them in your thinking and possibly facilitate expert help.

■ **Listen to people.** This can allow their anger to be defused. It is an important stage in them realizing that you have their interests at heart.

There are two tools that could help you. The first is to think **SAFE**: **S**eek to understand, **A**cknowledge emotions, **F**ocus on outcomes, **E**ncourage alternative behaviour. The secret is to focus on **S** and **A** before moving on. It works well with the boss.

The second tool involves drawing two squares:

1 In one box write your views on a given situation, using your perceptions and your logic.

2 In the other box write the views of the other, 'difficult' person, as you see them to be.

3 The third stage is to ask yourself how much these two boxes overlap and how much they differ.

If the boxes overlap totally, you won't be having a problem. If the boxes don't touch at all, you have a problem. Different cultures and beliefs need to be understood. First you need to understand each other; then work to increase the overlap between the two boxes.

Seek to be trusted before you seek to persuade or change.

overlapped slightly, and then we talked about why they overlapped so little. They came to understand each other and reached an accommodation that did at least allow them to work together without acrimony.

3.7

Allow for different cultures

I define culture as "the way we do things around here". You may need to spot differences of nationality, language or company style if you are to be on the same wavelength as someone else. This Secret shows you what to look for in respect of cultural differences.

■ **Develop knowledge, don't stereotype.** You should build on your experience with different cultures, but beware of pigeon-holing. In my book *Negotiating Secrets* there is a reference to the Japanese being very patient negotiators. Usually they are, but you should not be surprised if you come across some Japanese who will expect you to hurry up.
■ **Be aware of how culture has a real impact.** A study found that Britain's 'me culture' is the most individualistic in the world, valuing self over group. Whilst it makes for a dynamic and innovative popula-

> **case study** A subsidiary of a multinational asked for my help with people that the Operations Director labelled 'difficult'. I established that the problems outlined to me had not been fully discussed with the people concerned, even in their yearly appraisals. In

tion, it produces more depressed and unhappy people than more collectivist societies, such as China and Taiwan.

■ **Be careful with reputations.** Some jobs, such as share dealers, are known as being male-dominated, but this doesn't mean that you should anticipate an entirely macho environment.

■ **Understand company culture.** Some businesses have reputations for being very aggressive. If that is not your preferred style you may need to be aware of this if you are going for a job interview with them, or supplying them. Similarly, some businesses are strong on control (GE and GEC were good examples of that) whilst others encourage empowerment and the devolving of power. If you are to succeed in business, pick partners that suit your style.

■ **Manage your expectations.** Don't expect people to behave 'well' in your eyes. Expect them to be different and analyse those differences.

As someone who works in depth with a wide range of organizations, I have come across many different business cultures. Some encourage risk, others breed fear; some encourage bureaucracy and some encourage creativity. Sometimes culture is driven by the industry that they operate in. In aerospace, for instance, there is massive attention to detail. In many cases, the culture is dictated by the style of the Chief Exec. Whatever the situation, to avoid problems with difficult people, you need to allow for the culture in which they operate.

If you want to work harmoniously with people, allow for cultural differences.

their culture, feedback was not specific and not a valued part of their way of life. My feedback to the director was that these people were not the problem. The company culture was limiting performance, and he should take the lead in changing it.

3.8

Tailor relationships to suit the need

This Secret is about using skills to treat each person individually and each situation on its merits. It is the way to deliver results. It will also introduce you to a useful tool called Transactional Analysis.

Here are a few tips that will help you get the best from others.

■ **Don't focus on personality.** Don't seek to change an individual's personality, because you can't. Accept it and work with it.

■ **Focus on performance.** Pick specific behaviour, skills areas or knowledge that are affecting performance, and seek to change them.

■ **Treat your colleagues as if they were customers.** Imagine your colleagues, people in other departments and your boss to be customers. Give them the special attention that your real customers enjoy, but make the treatment suit their needs.

> **case study** Norman managed Ellin, who in turn managed a team of three, including Sue, who was shy. Ellin assumed an "I'm okay, you're okay" position with all her team. This would normally be considered good

Transactional Analysis (TA) was developed by Eric Berne, who wrote a book called *The Games People Play*. He suggested that we all fulfil different roles or states – we play a game. TA suggests that we are all a product of our experiences, and that this is at the heart of who we are and how we approach the building of relationships. TA is a big subject, but one of its concepts is that two people will work well together if they get to the state where they both feel, "I'm okay, and you're okay".

Here are a few tips on how to successfully tailor relationships:
■ **Performance.** Be driven by how effectively people perform rather than their personality. You can change performance, but not personality.
■ **Root cause.** Understand the root cause of the performance problem. Someone's behaviour is only a symptom, the tip of the iceberg.
■ **Risk.** Be aware of the balance between risk and reward. You need to be aware particularly of what happens if a high-risk strategy backfires.
■ **Change tack.** The golden rule is: if it's not working, change something. This is true of anything, from handling relationships to selling, negotiating and project managing.

Have a look at TA and decide where it fits in your toolkit.

practice, but in this case it didn't work because Sue did not see herself as okay. She saw herself as struggling and in need of support. It took Norman to point this out to Ellin before Sue contributed fully to the team.

Give difficult people a chance

How often are people difficult because they don't know where they are going, nor understand how important their contribution is to an organization? In this chapter we will give you tips on leadership, defining clear outcomes, roles and the communication needed to reinforce appropriate behaviour. These are crucial skills if you are a manager, but there is room for leadership at all levels. If leadership comes from you, there will be fewer difficult people around you!

4.1

Display leadership

There are many definitions of leadership. Some involve 'servant' leadership, which is less to do with shaping and more about helping people towards their goals. All definitions, though, involve some reference to the future. Here we look at how everyone needs to understand where their organization is going and see their part in its future.

Poor leadership will involve individuals not accepting their responsibilities and will result in difficult behaviour. There is a requirement for the organization to share with people a view of their future – defining their targets or outcomes is not enough. Even if you are not a line manager, there is a need for you to help people understand how the transactions that take place between you are an important part of moving the business forward and allowing all of you to be successful.

Leadership is a huge subject, and you would be well advised to study it, but here I will concentrate on a few tips that will reduce the number of difficult people around you.

one minute wonder Look for someone with whom you can share your view of the future right now.

"A leader shapes and shares a vision that others will follow"

Charles Handy, business visionary

■ **Consider situational leadership.** This is about varying your style to suit both the situation and the person you are dealing with. That means leaving behind your natural, or preferred, style and adopting one more appropriate to the specific situation that you find yourself in. For instance, you might naturally tend to delegate, whilst the situation could demand that you reassume responsibility for something. You may prefer detail to strategy, but the situation might demand that you attend to strategy. Be flexible.

■ **Act as a role model.** Foster the behaviour you want to see through your own behaviour – deliver on time, have consideration for others.

■ **Share the outcomes you are working towards.** Help those around you understand the outcomes you're after and appreciate what you seek to do and why.

■ **Pull together.** Create a common understanding of how best to achieve those outcomes and of the tasks and standards involved.

■ **Be responsible.** Accept responsibility for your own actions before you challenge others to do the same for theirs.

■ **Know when to be flexible.** Be consistent with regard to your approach to outcomes, but be flexible with regard to your communication and leadership style.

■ **Choose your battles.** Don't waste time on battles you can't win.

Effective leadership gives a clear direction, sets boundaries of responsibility and imparts a strong sense of what needs to be done. Whilst this gives people a sense of purpose, they will deliver most effectively if they can deliver in a way that suits them and the situation.

Is your leadership there for all to see?

4.2

Define clear outcomes

Defining positive outcomes is one of the most powerful things that organizations, teams and individuals can do. Do you know the key outcomes needed for you and those around you? Here's how to form outcomes and have fewer difficult people.

Creating outcomes reveals to everyone what the end game is, what they need to do, how they need to do it and whether they have the resources to do it. So, consider these points:

■ **How well defined are the outcomes?** For your organization, your team and you? Do the three fit together? Do they fit with the output of those around you? You may need to display leadership to align them.

case study As a young leader in retail, Alan found two long-serving, senior members of staff very difficult. They were not impressed by the fact that he was the boss and were unenthusiastic about what he asked them to do. Alan asked them why this was the case. They said, "Our previous manager always explained to

"Start with the end in mind"

Stephen Covey, 'The 7 Habits of Highly Effective People'

■ **Look at the KPIs.** The outcomes for the organization will be reflected in its KPIs (Key Performance Indicators) – for example, to make a 20% net profit within three years.

■ **Think about timescales.** To be useful to you, your outcomes should be a mix of goals: some short-term (e.g. skills); some medium-term (e.g. changes in your behaviour or decision-making); and others long-term (e.g. changes that you will bring about in your department).

■ **Make outcomes positive.** Saying what you don't want isn't very helpful, so agree what you do want to happen.

■ **Think SMART.** S is for Specific; M is for Measurable, so you can tell that it has happened; A is for Agreed, which means everyone involved needs to buy into it; R is for Realistic, otherwise it will demotivate people; and T is for Timed – when should it happen?

■ **Plan, do, review.** Clearly defined outcomes drive a healthy 'plan/do/review' culture, which will prompt regular reviews of the task, performance, skills, knowledge, process and resource.

■ **Difficult people or just a clash of roles?** The accounts team has to help control costs, and the marketing team needs to spend money!

Unless you want to be at everybody else's mercy, start with the end in mind.

us why we were doing things. You do things differently, and your priorities are difficult for us to understand." From then on Alan made sure that they knew what he was trying to achieve, and the context in which they were achieving it. As long as he gave them the big picture, they were quite happy.

4.3

Define clear roles and measures

How many people do you know with clearly defined job roles and measures of success? How many people look forward to constructive reviews of their performance? In my experience, they are in the minority. This Secret will motivate you and others by showing the importance of what you do.

There is a need to switch people on, and here's how to do it. I have written this as if you are the line manager, but these ideas can be used in discussion with anyone that you interact with.

■ **Instigate conversations about measures of success.** Unless you have to, don't bother with traditional bits of paper such as job descriptions. Concentrate instead on having a conversation with those around you about what kind of measures will show you that you have succeeded. In the case of sales people, these will include a sales figure. In the case of a receptionist it would include visitors feeling welcome. In the latter case you could conduct a survey of visitors. Another measure for the receptionist would be satisfied 'internal customers', so you would have to survey them to check on their satisfaction.

■ **Ascertain people's value to the business.** These measures are not difficult to agree, and they are totally job specific. They are not about what people do. They are about clarifying what each person's job delivers to the business. They make it clear to others what authority people have, because it is clear what outcomes they have to achieve. They are the job specification, so put them at the front of the performance review process.

■ **Measure the values of the business.** If the company has defined values, such as "we value teamwork", then measure teamwork!

■ **Create a person specification.** After the job specification, define the person specification by deciding the key attitudes, skills, knowledge and behaviours needed to succeed in each job. This need only take a few minutes, and it focuses the mind on the key competencies needed, which will help identify development needs.

■ **Share the process and results.** Openly share these measures with the team and those who work with the team. This is probably best done informally. It reveals the importance of each job, how dependent you are on each other and shows how jobs fit together.

■ **Find and sort out the problems.** Spot where there are contradictions or clashes of measures of success, and iron them out to reduce the number of difficult people and increase the number of switched-on people.

Use measures of success as a regular tool to motivate those around you.

4.4

Reward the right activities and results

What sort of rewards do you respond well to? When it comes to what motivates us and what turns us on, we are all different. Here we'll look at rewarding people for doing what is needed for the business, as well as flagging up to people the consequences of activity that is out of line with the business needs.

Let us assume that you are all aware of the outcomes needed, and everybody knows how to get there. Is that enough? No, because things will crop up to blow you off course. What you need to do with the people around you, including your boss, is to reward them when they do the right things and have them do appropriate things.

Opposite are some rewards that might reinforce the right things that you see being done and encourage people to focus on their measures of success and driving the business forward.

case study I encountered a PR business in which outcomes were not clearly defined, departmental responsibilities were not aligned and tasks were tackled in a chaotic fashion. As a result very creative

■ **Praise.** You can use praise one-on-one, in team meetings and in written communications, including email. Public praise is especially powerful.
■ **Trust.** Some people see being allowed to exercise their discretion as a reward, so leave dependable people alone with a minimum of reviews.
■ **Promotion.** Extra responsibility could encourage many to keep moving in the right direction.
■ **Money.** Some are driven by financial rewards, like salary or bonuses.

There are countless rewards that will keep good practice going. They include saying "thank you," being encouraging, devoting your time to someone, helping them develop and giving extra challenges. Your job is to see the right things happening and reward the individual as appropriate. These things are so much easier if they are a part of the culture in which you operate, and if reviewing performance is a way of life.

Every bit as important is the need to intervene if you see things happening that are not relevant to the business. The quicker you do this, the less likely you are to end up with a difficult person; put it off, and it could become a big problem. Highlight the consequences of irrelevant action, because frequently this is a blind spot to people.

Reward anyone doing the things that drive the organization forward.

people worked on the tasks that they preferred, rather than what they should have been doing. After discussion, the director accepted the significance of this and focused on doing what was needed!

4.5

Reinforce appropriate behaviour

The previous Secret focused on rewarding the right activity. Here we'll look at reinforcing appropriate behaviour – that is, the *way* things are done rather than what is being done. Use both Secrets together to minimize the number of difficult people.

This Secret and the previous one have a big thing in common. They are both about rewarding and reinforcing what it is that you want in the business. Once again, this is easier if there is leadership from the top, and it is part of the culture – but your isolated contribution to reinforcing the right behaviour will help develop improved relationships with those around you.

case study Norman was coaching a manager who had constant problems in meetings with two people. They undermined what was going on, which distracted the others. Norman suggested that the manager might try several things with the two difficult people – have separate chats with them to understand

■ **Work on values.** Make sure that company values are not just posted on the noticeboard and forgotten. That will make them a waste of time. Encourage company values to be identified and for the associated behaviours to be reinforced. So, if one of your values is "We value team before self", make sure that the behaviours that look like good teamwork are privately and publicly reinforced and rewarded.

■ **Manage performance.** Incorporate the above ideas into your performance review process, so that you will review behaviours as a way of life and also periodically review values-based behaviour.

■ **Reward.** Use praise, trust, promotion, money and other rewards to reinforce the behaviours that you have identified as important.

■ **Ground rules.** If you are engaged in meetings, a project team or a new relationship with someone, you would be advised to agree ground rules at the start. I do this when working with a new team, and it produces items like, "Listen to each other" or "Switch off mobile phones." Agreeing them is the easy bit; the real value comes from reinforcing them so that everyone functions effectively. Amend them as and when necessary to make sure that they continue to fit your need.

■ **Be consistent.** If you're not, you're asking for trouble!

■ **Be balanced.** As well as addressing inappropriate behaviour, be sure that those around you realize that you appreciate them for being them.

Will you reinforce the behaviours that you want to see?

why they were behaving in this way, establish a few ground rules, and thank them or praise them when their behaviour helped the meeting move forward. The manager chose to do all three. Within two weeks he was able to say that behaviours had been turned round, and the meetings had become very productive.

4.6

Communicate with a clear purpose

This is a massive subject and much of this book is about how to communicate. What we'll particularly focus on here is the different aspects of communication that affect your dealings with difficult people, and offer you tips for key areas.

There is a purpose to communication, so firstly be clear what it is. Keep going until you have crystallized it. Here's how:

■ **Clarify.** When dealing with difficult people, ensure that they are in no doubt about how you feel, what you expect and the consequences of them not changing. Make sure they can never legitimately say, "I didn't know that" or "You didn't tell me that".

> **case study** A client wanted a fresh approach in his company. Staff had been poorly informed about business performance, and we chose to use the Industrial Society model for Team Briefs. The Chief Executive prepared a monthly brief on company performance that went to four directors. They each added their

"The ear of any leader must ring with the voices of the people"

Woodrow Wilson, US President 1913–21

■ **Choose your style.** Reid and Merrill identified four social styles and the way to communicate with each. *Drivers* want it to the point; *Amiables* want it to be all about people's needs; *Analysts* want the facts; *Expressives* want enthusiasm. Match your approach to theirs.

■ **Listen.** Before speaking, seek to understand them and their situation.

■ **Start big.** As on TV news, start with the headlines – tell them what the story is about before you give them the detail.

■ **Choose your medium.** Do you need to write a letter or is an email more appropriate? Will your body language be important? Is the message so crucial that you need to say it face-to-face?

■ **Check timing.** Tackling problems early is usually better than later; nip fears in the bud; little and often is better than a big fuss.

■ **Organize team Briefs.** These are a good way of cascading information down through an organization.

■ **Harness power.** Knowledge is power, so make sure that no one is hogging it. Spread knowledge through the business.

Whatever your position, communicate, communicate, communicate.

notes on departmental performance before forwarding a brief that went to each of their team leaders. The team leaders took the key bits of this information and added their own view when they briefed their teams. That way the entire company was briefed on company performance as well as their team performance.

Use the right tool for the situation

In this chapter you will find skills for tackling each situation on its own merits. And by giving each person individual attention, you will hopefully develop a rapport. We'll look at how to diagnose the right problem and choose the best tool for a given situation. We will look at how to organize feedback and make use of business systems to support your case. We will also look at psychometric tests, which might help you find common ground with a difficult person.

5.1

Dig out the data

What is the real problem? Unless you define the problem properly you will merely paper over the cracks; you won't solve it. Here we look at how to gather the data and facts that will ensure that you address the real problem and not just the symptoms.

The key to making sure that you address the right problem is asking lots of questions. Here are Kipling's six, from the quote above:

■ **What?** What is the problem? What is the scale of the problem? What is the larger problem? What data do you need to solve it?
■ **Why?** Why is this a problem? Why has the problem occurred? Why has no one solved it?
■ **When?** When does it show itself? When was it first spotted?

case study The case study in Secret 1.6 is a good example of a situation in which snap judgements about the bullying Sales Director were unhelpful. We only got to the bottom of the matter, and established that he was an alcoholic, by several of us collaborating in gathering information about what was happening and when. We pooled several pieces of data, which

> "I kept six honest serving men, they taught me all I knew. Their names are What and Why and When and Where and How and Who."

Rudyard Kipling, English author

■ **How?** How did the problem first show itself? How does it affect performance? How effective were previous solutions?

■ **Where?** Where did it originate and where does it impact?

■ **Who?** Who is responsible and who is affected?

The key to gathering all the facts is to treat the difficult person as you would any other problem. One of my favourite tools for addressing soft problems is force field analysis, which involves you asking:

1 Where you are now? (State A)
2 Where do you want to get to? (State B)
3 What are the forces that will help you get from A to B?
4 What are the forces preventing you moving from A to B?
5 How will you use the forces for, and overcome the forces against, in order to resolve the problem.

First things first: gather the facts.

were not known by all of us, in order to see the pattern. He regularly took Mondays off after boozy weekends; he drank excessively at work functions; he had two car accidents despite priding himself on his driving; and he plundered the drinks cabinet in the dining room. Only by gathering the facts together did we have enough to persuade him that he needed specialist help.

5.2

Diagnose the problem

Once you have gathered the data, you have to diagnose the real problem and consider your options before investing time and effort in a solution. Once again, you can use classic diagnostic tools, three of which are described below.

1 **Force field analysis.** This looks at 'helping forces' and 'hindering forces' (see previous Secret). It helps you ask the right questions and gather data to reveal the real problem.

2 **Fishbone diagram.** This is a diagram with a line and 'fishbone' spikes. It helps you see how various factors are interacting to form a problem.

3 **Why? Why?** This approach depends on you drilling deeper and deeper by constantly asking "why?". It goes like this: "Why is Lucy constantly late?" She misses the bus. "Why does she miss the bus?" She leaves too little time for the walk to the bus stop. "Why does she…" Keep asking "why?" and you will diagnose the problem.

one minute wonder When you next encounter a difficult person (a) ask yourself how tough you can afford to be, and (b) ask why they are being difficult.

Any differences between two people are a potential problem. You might seek to reduce the differences, or you might find a way to accept them. Either way, it will help to spot what might be the root cause. We have discussed a few, and here are a few more:

■ **Language.** I don't just mean a foreign language, but the irritation that comes from one person speaking theoretically or conceptually, whilst someone else speaks in practical terms.

■ **Fragile or tough-minded.** Mental toughness can be considered as the capability of an individual to cope with pressures, stress and severe challenges. Some people have this while others don't, and this can change with circumstances. Your judgement of why someone is how they are, and what they are capable of changing about themselves, is an important part of your diagnosis.

■ **Style.** Any clash of style can represent a problem, be it audio or visual, introvert or extrovert, negative or positive, open or inhibited, pleasant or unpleasant. You need to ask what has caused these differences before you can decide what it will take to bridge the gap.

■ **Illness.** You are not a trained counsellor but you need to be on the look out for physical or mental illness, or domestic problems that could necessitate the introduction of professional help.

Don't rush to apportion blame. Do the diagnosis to find the real problem.

5.3

Decide if there is a task-related issue

This Secret is about keeping it simple, and not over-complicating the solution. It is important to do a full diagnosis, but there is no need to dive into behavioural issues if there is a simple, task-related problem.

Rather than dig into the character and background of the difficult person, first look for some of the things that need to be right to give the pair of you a chance. Is the task not getting done because of what surrounds the pair of you? If there are any gaps, plug these first. One gap could involve the question of direction. Does your difficult person know where the company is going? Do they have **SMART** targets (see also Secret 4.2)?

---

case study I was coaching a manager who was struggling with a team of 10 development engineers. She was very technical, and so were they. All of them tended to ignore leadership and management issues, but tensions between them were high and they did not cooperate with each other. We put in place an awareness of where the business was going, how their

---

S is for **Specific** so they know what they have to deliver.
M is for **Measurable** so that they know when they have succeeded.
A is for **Agreed**, which means that everyone who is involved in helping that person deliver is fully committed to that target.
R is for **Realistic**. Ask yourself: "Can it be done?" "Is it challenging?"
T is for **Timed**, so that they know when they have to deliver it.

Here are a few more to look out for:

■ Is there a supportive 'plan/do/review' procedure in place?
■ Have you exchanged expectations of how you will work together?
■ Are there satisfactory communication links with other people and other departments? Is the necessary information there?

There is sometimes a case for taking the trouble to write down what you have agreed and what you are doing. This isn't for legalistic reasons, but to demonstrate that you care and to show that you are organized. Attending to these basics may solve the problem with a minimum of fuss and avoid it escalating into a more antagonistic and intractable situation.

Ask yourself - what is stopping the task from getting done?

team's contribution was critical to the company's future, and instigated SMART targets for all of them, including the manager. She presented her targets for discussion alongside everyone else's. The transformation was remarkable. That was five years ago and the lady concerned has been promoted and is still using these principles as a way of running her team.

5.4

Form a psychological contract

The contract between employee and employer is much more than what is written on paper. It is also about the perception of the two parties. Here we will extend the idea of a contract into the perceptions of any two people who work together; it's a powerful way to avoid difficulties and improve performance.

What we expect of each other is sometimes informal and imprecise; it is about our unwritten obligations towards each other. What does each party expect and what does each party promise, without necessarily spelling it out?

case study With most of my customers, I have an exchange of expectations with them at the offset. With Stuart, a sales manager, we had a very clear exchange. Here is part of what Stuart expected of me: to understand his needs; to give him practical advice on field sales management; to speak his language; to give him honest feedback and always ring him on his mobile.

"A piece of paper is not a contract; it is merely evidence of a contract" Sam, my lawyer

■ **Employees.** They might expect fair pay, opportunities for development or promotion, respect, a package of benefits, etc.

■ **Employers.** They could expect people to turn up on time, demonstrate commitment and effort, plus flexibility and loyalty.

■ **Both.** Employers and employees promise certain things by their actions or by what they say during recruitment, conversations or reviews. Though not written down, the actions and words form a psychological contract between employee and employer that has a profound effect on the way they work together.

If we accept that we have a psychological contract with everyone with whom we interface at work, we can improve relationships and reduce the incidence of 'difficult' people. You need to have conversations with people about what they expect of you and what you expect of them. This contract needs to be constantly updated between you to cater for the changing situations.

Be aware of the unwritten agreements that exist in the workplace.

Among the things that I expected were for him to make time for his development; to tell me what was confidential; to share the learning with his manager; to help me make it practical; to give me honest feedback and never to ring me on my mobile. We still work well together after 10 years, and we never stop checking each other's expectations.

5.5

Use third-party feedback

Feedback from a third party can greatly help you if you are trying to show someone that it is in their own interests to change their behaviour. Here are a few suggestions as to how you can incorporate third-party feedback into your toolkit and so improve a difficult working relationship.

This Secret and the next are about using feedback from others to help you influence someone to change their behaviour. Third-party feedback is a particularly useful device to have in your tool kit for solving problems that involve two opposing views. It can help enable you to persuade and influence the people around you to change what they do.

However persuasive you may be, there are occasions when it is difficult for you to persuade another person that they need to change. Someone else (a third party) might show them what is needed, perhaps by using different words or maybe because they have a certain chemistry with them.

> **"The greatest discovery of my generation is that human beings can alter their lives by altering their attitude of mind"** William James, psychologist

As always, use this idea in a way that suits the situation:

■ **Getting consent.** The third-party approach will only work if the person with whom you are having difficulty is open to the idea. Pressurizing someone to do it will simply make things worse.

■ **Impartiality.** The process works best when the third party is seen to be impartial. One of the benefits of an impartial third party is that they may come up with ideas that suggest that you are as much of a problem as the other person in the conflicted relationship. The third party should not apportion blame, but merely help the relationship improve.

■ **Outcomes.** Agree among the three of you just what you all expect to finish up with. Is it merely to identify the problem for now? Or are you seeking to find a solution to the problem?

■ **Role.** Make sure that everyone involved understands the role of the third party – expert, adjudicator, mediator, observer or facilitator?

■ **Style.** Is it to be formal or informal; written down or purely verbal?

■ **Who?** It could be your boss; it could be someone who works with both of you; it could be someone from outside your organization.

■ **Credibility.** The person concerned has to be respected, credible and seen to be trustworthy by both parties.

Be aware of the value of a third party for offering an objective view.

5.6

Use 360-degree feedback

This is an extension of using third-party feedback, except you organize feedback from several people who have a relationship with the person in question. A manager could organize this for one of her team, or you could organize feedback focused on yourself. This is a powerful tool that generates positive ideas.

Let's say we are looking at the leadership qualities of Julie, and we are using 360-degree feedback to help with her Personal Development Plan. Follow these steps:

1 **Form criteria.** Identify the criteria that are important in Julie's job, and ask people to rate her with regard to each of those qualities. If leadership is involved, you might ask people to rate Julie's ability to: (A) shape and share a vision; (B) think strategically; (C) demonstrate commitment to agreed plans. I use a form on leadership that has 24 such criteria. For each of the criteria, ask people to rate Julie from 1 = Not at all, through to 6 = Always, with comments to support each rating.

2 **Seek agreement.** Before you use the form you have to make sure that Julie is happy for the form to be distributed to a chosen group of people – about five to ten, including her boss, some colleagues and people from other departments. Usually the responses are confidential and fed back to one person, who collates the feedback.

3 **Give a clear brief.** The group has to be briefed as to how the process will work, and how they should fill in the form.

4 **Include self-assessment.** Julie should rate herself from 1 to 6 with regard to each of the qualities.

5 **Compare the results.** When the results are collated, they are presented to Julie, and you can compare her view of herself with other people's views of her.

This is a powerful and rigorous assessment tool, so make sure you take into account the following points:

■ **Balance the views.** Julie needs to see the whole process as being about spotting her strengths as well as her development need, or she will disengage and feel picked on – as would you!

■ **Support the person.** There are likely to be some shocks for Julie, so she needs to feel supported. Spend more time supporting Julie afterwards than you spent on designing the process.

■ **Inform the other parties.** Thank the people who gave feedback and, if it's okay with Julie, explain the outcome to them.

360-degree feedback can be a very powerful development tool.

5.7

Create a common framework

Here we'll look at sharing a concept, a framework or a business model with the people around you. It can give teams a focal point, change the culture of a company even, and it bridges gaps between people.

Not only can a common framework and shared ethos overcome difficulties and create unity, it can even stop them arising in the first place. Here are just three examples:

■ **Team roles.** In the Secret that follows we will look at Belbin team roles, which describe preferred team roles such as 'Plant' and 'Shaper'. Plants are great with ideas, but they can be difficult to organize. Once you appreciate the term and see how the role can fit, you'll know when Plant behaviour is helpful and when it's likely to be a problem.

case study A project team designed a performance management system that linked 'mission', 'values' 'competencies', and 'company and individual performance'. The package produced a shared language to describe and manage performance. The behaviour

■ **Competence.** If you all know that in your organization there is a requirement to behave in a certain way, it becomes easier to talk about behaviour. If your company values teamwork, for example, a code that includes "put team before self" will show what's needed. When someone puts themselves before the team, it is easier to raise the issue.

■ **Models.** One of my favourite models involves the triangle below. The top third represents **Task**, the middle third **Process** and the bottom third **Feelings**. The idea is that, in most organizations, the emphasis is on task, and it is only if there is a problem with the task that anyone looks at process, and only a serious problem will tempt anyone to ask what feelings are stopping the processes from kicking in. The model doesn't say that feelings are all important, but it does suggest you look at it the other way round. If you start by understanding the feelings in a company, the processes will kick in and the task will get done.

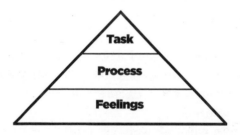

Find a framework that will give you a common understanding.

identified as desirable for all employees to display included: a readiness to learn; an endeavour to be creative; and a consideration for profitability. So, if someone failed to act in a cost-conscious fashion, for example, it was easy for colleagues to take them to task.

5.8

Promote dialogue

Meredith Belbin identified several key roles within a team. Understand them and you will contribute more to any team, and manage a team better. Here are six of Belbin's key ideas:

1 There are different roles that need to be performed in any team.
2 We all have preferred roles that we like to adopt. They are not necessarily what we are good at; we just prefer them.
3 We can only be good at performing two or three of these roles.
4 An effective team will have balance, with each of these roles being fulfilled by someone.
5 Different roles will clash with each other.
6 Each role is important at different stages of a project, because they have different strengths and weaknesses.

case study I used Belbin analysis on The Post Office management development team to promote greater understanding of how their teams were performing. Each team member filled out a questionnaire, giving a score for each of the key roles outlined above. The whole team could then see the roles that each person liked best and least. We looked at each person in turn,

The key roles identified by Belbin are:

■ **Plants** are creative, ideas people, and often poor communicators.
■ **Resource investigators** explore opportunities. They are extrovert, but can lose interest quickly.
■ **Co-ordinators** tie together the activities of various team members. They are good all rounders, not stars.
■ **Shapers** force action and get results, but they can upset others.
■ **Monitor evaluators** consider matters, check everything is on track and are seldom inspirational.
■ **Team workers** support others, are sociable, but do not lead.
■ **Implementers** do what needs doing; practical but can be inflexible.
■ **Completer finishers** finish things, usually on their own. They fulfil promises, but can worry about trivial things.
■ **Specialists** provide particular skills that they are immersed in, so they contribute on a narrow front.

Belbin's ideas will help you understand your other team members and cope with the different types in your team. The case study gives examples of how you might use these ideas to improve your own performance or the performance of your team.

Accept that different types are needed in a successful team.

and asked for examples of how their behaviour at work fitted their profile. We agreed how sometimes a team member's behaviour needed to be tolerated, how sometimes they needed to change and how the team as a whole could be strengthened. As an example, some teams were light on Plants, so activities to generate ideas had to be introduced.

5.9

Understand conflict

A tool developed by K.W. Thomas and R.H. Kilmann will give you a useful insight into how you and others tackle conflict – or avoid it. This is an overview of their approach. If used well, it could save you a great deal of hassle and lots of money.

Thomas and Kilmann (T-K) identified five basic conflict-handling modes that we use. They are:

1 **Competing.** This is uncooperative, with people pursuing their own interests at other people's expense.

2 **Accommodating.** The opposite of competing, this is a self-sacrificing response, yielding to the views of others.

3 **Avoiding.** This is when someone sidesteps an issue, or withdraws from a threat.

4 **Collaborating.** The opposite of avoiding, this is about exploring what satisfies the concerns of both parties.

5 **Compromising.** This is the middle ground between competing and accommodating.

"Bring your opponents to their senses and not to their knees"

Mahatma Ghandi

You can make use of the T-K Instrument (TKI) simply to understand yourself, to work on it with one other person, or to look at it as a team. However you use it, you can increase self awareness, develop the awareness of others, assess conflict situations and develop your skills.

■ Secure the literature, including the questionnaires, and fill in the form. This can be done online via www.kilmann.com.

■ Use the associated workbook to understand what your own preferred style is. T-K suggest that we are usually only comfortable in one or two of the five styles.

■ Look at the results for your difficult person, or your team, and ask if their preferences explain their approach to conflict.

■ Look at specific examples of conflict between you, and explore how you can work better together.

■ Ask yourself, and others, if there is a need to expand the styles that you are comfortable with – if, for instance, there is a need to collaborate when your natural inclination is to avoid.

■ Accept some differences in style, but be aware of the need to change your approach.

There are several alternative conflict models that you can access on the Internet and through licence holders. Whatever you choose to do, don't avoid the issue!

Understand conflict and keep working on your conflict-handling skills.

5.10

Use psychometric profiling

Psychometric tests can clarify your perspective on a difficult person or relationship. We have looked at two already in the previous two Secrets and later we'll look at Honey and Mumford's learning styles (Secret 7.1). These are all psychometric tests that identify people's preferences and help us understand their behaviour.

There are many different kinds of psychometric profiling tests available. Merrill and Reid, for example, analyse behaviour in terms of **social styles**, such as 'drivers', 'expressives', 'amiables' and 'analyticals'. Other methods focus more on the individual, through **personality profiles**. Widely used tests of this kind include: MBTI (Myers-Briggs

case study Sue asked me for a second opinion on a candidate for the position of her sales director. I interviewed him, and at the end of the session felt uneasy about whether he was being straightforward about his motives for wanting the job and whether he was an open enough character to fit in with Sue's team. I

Type Indicator); OPQ (Occupational Personality Questionnaire) and 16PF (which uses 16 Personality Factors). **Aptitude and skill tests** could also help you understand why someone is presenting difficulties. Tests of verbal, keyboard or numerical skills could help you diagnose a performance problem.

All these tests can be used in the selection process or to uncover the reasons for poor performance. There are plenty of 'dos and don'ts':

■ **Don't expect definite answers.** No test can deliver a definitive answer. They need to be used in conjunction with other data, such as performance reviews, feedback and interviews (see case study).

■ **Tread carefully.** Don't overestimate your ability to use any test, as you are making judgements on other people's personality and perform-ance. If in doubt, use a licensed practitioner for a particular tool.

■ **Match your approach to the problem.** Most tools have a specific use, so use different tools to tackle different situations.

■ **Keep everyone on-side.** Pay attention to how the results are received. You don't want a testee to resent both you and the process!

Find a test that best suits the situation.

enlisted the help of Norman Leet, who suggested we use the 16PF questionnaire. Two big question marks arose from the results over motivation and sociability. I suggested Sue have another chat with him, focusing on these two issues. She did, and it confirmed her uneasiness. Sue made the decision not to recruit him.

Develop
your skills

This chapter looks at your general approach to business, and how you can build on everyday skills to manage difficult situations that might arise. We will focus on how to visualize success; give feedback to others; use effective body language; contribute positively to meetings; really connect with people; and use your power to influence others.

6.1

Visualize success

Visualizing success means just that – planting a picture in your head of what success would look like. This affects your subconscious in such a way that you are more likely to do what's necessary to achieve success.

In recent years, the idea of using a positive image of what you want to achieve has been incorporated into NLP (Neuro Linguistic Programming). Here's how to do it:

1 Create a clear picture of a specific goal that you want to achieve. It might be to do with holing a putt at golf; playing happily with your children; having a certain amount of money in the bank; or working harmoniously with someone!

2 Close your eyes and imagine, like Einstein, what success looks like. Picture it! Make the picture as clear as possible, with details of people, size, colour and actions – like a dream.

case study This example is a sporting one, but it can be just as powerful for you in business. Many top sportsmen use this tool. When Nick Faldo was winning his major golf titles, he used to warm up on the range. Except he didn't! He was visualizing his way around

"Imagination is everything. It is the preview of life's coming attractions" **Albert Einstein**

3 Feel the emotions of that success. Are you happy, relieved, proud, relaxed, or what?

4 Do this repeatedly, for a few minutes twice a day until you succeed.

5 Help the process by keeping hard copy pictures of what you want, or notes that describe what a successful relationship will look like. I keep a picture of Tom Watson's golf swing on my office wall, because it shows a position of the left arm that I need to match.

How does this work with someone who is presenting difficulties? Go through the above process, and specifically:

■ **Imagine a scenario.** Think about a situation in which you are happily sitting together, smiling and talking.

■ **Create a picture.** Fix a clear picture of what they will be doing with you: shaking hands with you, for example, or saying "thank you".

■ **Visualize success.** In your head, envisage the results of your success: the two of you working together on a problem, the two of you exchanging information, outsiders admiring you, etc.

To help you succeed, close your eyes and imagine.

the golf course that he was about to play. He visualized his first tee shot, and his second... He visualized the chips. On the putting green, he visualized the putts he would make on the course, the adjustments to his swing. Try it – the visualization, not the golf swing!

6.2

Give helpful feedback

We all learn from feedback, whether it's from others or internal. Feedback drives improved performance. I am going to offer you a framework that will make it easy for you to give others feedback in any situation.

One of the golden rules of feedback is to deliver it as soon as possible after the event – the impact is diminished if you put it off.

I was given the **EEC** framework for feedback by an associate called Andrew Lawless. EEC is based on the idea that when giving people feedback it is important that they understand (a) what they did, (b) what the effect was, and (c) what they need to continue or change.

■ **E = Example.** Tell the person exactly what they did. This should be as specific as possible about what they did. It should be relevant, supportive, helpful and clear.

case study Liz is one of Lee's suppliers. She prides herself on her networking. However, Lee and some of his colleagues began to feel irritable with the constant phone calls and questions, although no one dared to tell Liz that she was overdoing it. One day Lee decided to offer EEC: "Liz, you rang me up yesterday, asked me

> **"Any fool can criticize, condemn, and complain – and most fools do"** Dale Carnegie, American self-help guru

■ **E = Effect.** Tell them the effect of their actions on you. This will relate to how it made you feel. It is difficult for someone to take offence at how you feel, because it's not an attack on them! Your feelings can be either negative or positive. Again, be as specific as possible.

■ **C = Continue or Change.** For your feedback to be taken seriously, plenty of it needs to be positive! If your feedback is positive and the individual is not required to do anything different in future, your feedback sounds like "thanks" or "please keep this up". If the feedback is to change, agree with them how to make a change. This should be based on you suggesting ways in which they can change their behaviour. For example, "I wish you would…", or "Please make sure that…" Whether it's continue or change, check if your feedback is accepted.

EEC makes your life easy because 'E' for Effect avoids you getting personal. It's when your feedback gets personal or judgemental that you will stir up bad feeling. Avoid saying, "Your attitude is wrong."

If you want to change the behaviour of those around you, use EEC feedback.

lots of questions and explained what you were doing. I have to say that I felt as though you were working me like you work a machine. I wish that after all the time we've known each other your approach would be more relaxed." It was a difficult point to make, but Liz took it well and later thanked Lee for the feedback.

6.3

Encourage feedback from others

Feedback from others allows you to learn something valuable about the impact you have on the world. Do other people's perceptions of you line up with what you intended? Here is how you check that out, and improve your act – however good it is.

If other people's perception matches what you want, keep it up. If not, avoid the temptation to defend yourself. Remember, it may not be easy for the giver either, so don't make it more difficult for them!

■ **Listen quietly.** No interruptions, no escaping into defensive strategy – just concentrate on what is being said and mentally note questions or disagreements that occur to you.

> **case study** As a young manager I worked closely with Manish, an accountant, setting up a distribution system for motorcycle spares. When Manish was leaving the company, he said to me: "You're a perfectionist; I'll miss you." I said automatically, "Thank you, that's very kind of you." "Hang on," he said, "that wasn't entirely a

> "It's a rare person who wants to hear what he doesn't want to hear" **Dick Cavett, chat show host**

■ **Reflect back.** Summarize to check that you got the intended messages and to show that you are listening. Their views are valid, even if you do not think they are correct.

■ **Explore.** You may not agree with what you hear, but try to *understand* what is being said and why this person is reacting in this way. Stay calm, show interest and seek examples to clarify.

■ **Ask for more.** Remember, sincere feedback should help you, not get at you, so ask for more feedback about other things that you do.

■ **Express your honest reactions.** This includes feelings – you don't have to keep it all bottled up, but try not to be defensive or aggressive.

■ **Thank them.** You owe them this but don't feel pressured to act against your judgement or reciprocate by saying something nice (or nasty!) back.

When receiving feedback, as in giving feedback, leave the rational thinking and problem-solving till the end, when all the emotion has dissipated. Listen first, then solve the problem. Finally, make choices about what, if anything, you will change in your behaviour.

Treat feedback to you as an opportunity for you to overcome obstacles.

compliment. That was feedback too! Your obsession with getting everything perfect has made working with you extremely difficult, and slowed us down!" Manish was right, and I resolved to curb this tendency, helped by other colleagues who gave me feedback on how I was doing. I think it's under control!

6.4

Know the significance of body language

Body language is a crucial aspect of communicating. It is a huge subject, and all I seek to do here is alert you to its significance, and show you that it is to your advantage to look into it further if you want to win people round.

Research has shown that 10% of your message depends on the words you use, 30% on how you say them and 60% on your body language. You need to read other people's body language, decide what it is telling you and use your body language positively. Here are a few examples.

■ **Eye contact.** If someone looks at you for only 30% of the time, consider that they might be lying or hiding something. If their eye contact is more than 70% it could mean that they find you interesting, or that they are being hostile.

■ **The eye rub.** This can indicate lying, but women might rub their eye to avoid making a violent gesture, or they might just have an itch!

■ **The handshake.** A crushing handshake could be a sign that this person is going to start aggressively.

■ **Arms crossed.** Crossed arms could show the same thing, or rejection of your point.

■ **Palm gestures.** Both palms facing upwards could be a sign of openness.

Don't read too much into body language until you have studied it in greater depth (see further reading). You might think that someone who refuses to look you in the eye is lying. That could be a dangerous assumption, but if you see a man rubbing his eye or pulling his collar, avoiding your eye and shifting uneasily in their chair, then it's quite likely they are lying. Finally, be aware that some people do not give favourable first impressions, but under the surface could be real talent.

Here are a few tips to help you build good rapport with those around you:

■ **Be conscious of the first impression you create.** People form 90% of their impression of you in the first 90 seconds.

■ **Use people's names with a smile.** First, check how they would like to be addressed.

■ **Avoid sitting directly opposite someone.** This applies especially at a square or rectangular table. Ideally sit at 60 degrees at a round table.

■ **Lean forward.** This creates the impression that you are interested in what is being said. Establish eye contact about 60–70% of the time. More than that is intimidating in most cultures.

■ **Shake hands with a comfortable pressure.** Make it not too strong, but not feeble.

■ **Don't invade people's personal space.** A metre apart is about as close as you should get.

Recognize that how you say something and your body language are often more important than the words themselves.

6.5

Get results from meetings

Poorly managed meetings produce disengaged, disenchanted and difficult people. As with other situations, sometimes it is our own approach that causes people to be difficult in meetings. Here we will look at how to take the stress out of meetings and reduce the risk of people becoming difficult.

I will avoid duplicating conventional wisdom. Instead, I will pass on some tips that will help you with difficult people and stop you becoming difficult yourself.

If you are attending a meeting

■ **Establish expectations.** Know in advance what is expected of you.
■ **Be equipped.** Make sure that you have the necessary attitudes, skills and knowledge needed for the meeting. Secure the necessary coaching or training to allow you to shine.
■ **Pre-position.** If you know of anyone who will present you with difficulties in the meeting, have a prior meeting with them to iron out any differences between you.

■ **Lobby the participants.** If you see difficulties with regard to a particular person or subject, check out beforehand what support you are likely to receive from others.

If you are chairing or managing the meeting

1 Make sure that everyone knows what is expected of them before they turn up.
2 Before starting, remind people of the outputs needed, and the behavioural ground rules for success.
3 Avoid having the same set of people attending the same meetings for the whole time. Instead, create a situation where the group trust each other to handle some things in their absence. Develop a culture where there is no stigma attached to not attending. If people only attend those items that affect them, they will save a great deal of wasted time and money.
4 Consider how to involve the whole group. One way to encourage this is to rotate the roles of chairperson, minute-taker, timekeeper and controller of interruptions.
5 Ask the minute-taker to make notes in the form of action points, by whom, and by when. Photocopy this before the meeting ends, and secure everyone's agreement to the actions. Alternatively, if the minutes are typed on a laptop, have them printed and agreed before everyone disperses. It is rare for minutes to cover a legal requirement, so this minimalist approach to minutes is a huge time saver and also reduces the likelihood of problems in the future.
6 After a meeting, reinforce positive behaviour by giving people feedback on their contribution.

Put a bit of extra thought into any meeting where you anticipate difficulty with someone.

6.6

Look at timelines

Timelines are a fresh way of looking at what you are involved in, and they can help you unlock the mystery of a difficult person or a tricky situation. This secret looks at what timelines actually are and how you can use them as part of your skill set.

A simple timeline is just a line on a piece of paper, with a description of where you are at one end and a description of where you want to get to at the other. It's your journey. Here are a few examples – use them to help you understand what you are trying to achieve.

■ **Outcomes.** Draw a line sloping upwards. At the bottom left, describe your present situation. At the top right, describe where you want to finish up. Between these two endpoints you can mark goals, milestones and the resources that you need. You can define any problem as the difference between the present and future states.

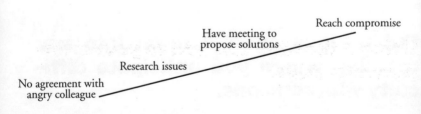

Reach compromise

Have meeting to
propose solutions

Research issues

No agreement with
angry colleague

■ **Relationships.** The same principle applies to any relationship that you seek to improve. Bottom left: describe your present state in terms of behaviours, thoughts and feelings. Top right: describe your future state through the behaviours, thoughts and feelings that you want to achieve. Along the way you can put milestones and identify what tools you will use and what help you might need. Paint a visual picture of both states, and visualize success.

■ **Spot different thinking.** Some people see time in front of them. They like progress; they stay on track; they may function poorly in chaos; they need to finish; they are not focused on the here and now. Others can focus in chaos; they like things open-ended; they love the here and now. If someone lives in the past, your timeline can start with how it was! Match people's language in order to get the best out of them. Sometimes you will seek to change their behaviour, but first of all you have to spot the difference.

Timelines can help you decide where you are currently heading in your career, or where you really want to be going. Some people also find timelines a useful tool in project management.

Using a timeline can add to your inter-personal skills.

6.7

Get personal

What do I mean by getting personal? I don't mean delving into the intimate details of somebody's life. I mean creating a bridge between their world and yours to create trust and effective communication.

To work with someone, you have to develop a rapport with them. You don't have to agree with them, but respond to them in such a way that they feel understood. Here are some ways to achieve this.

■ **Be face-to-face with them.** Beware of relying too much on emails and memos. Our look at body language stressed the importance of the human touch. In this electronic age we make dangerous assumptions about how vast amounts of information are interpreted and about the message that is received. Humans need human contact.

■ **'Stroke' them gently.** Communications don't always have to be heavy and powerful. Light 'strokes' have an important and cumulative effect. So a "good morning", the odd smile through the day, the occasional "thank you" and "safe journey home" all have a part to play.

one minute wonder Try some of these ideas on your friends before trying them at work.

"To communicate effectively, we first have to realize we are all different" Anthony Robbins, advisor to world leaders

■ **Match them.** Try matching their body language, and the style and tone of their language. In fact, if you match anything that they do, they will consciously or subconsciously feel that you are entering their world. You can do this with your posture, facial expressions, eye movements and hand movements. The tone of your voice and the volume can change the way your message is received. Try experimenting.

■ **Pace yourself with them.** Match the speed of their speech, or the speed of their body movement. You are unlikely to get a brilliant response from someone who is doing everything slowly if you dash past them full of energy. I'm not asking you to mimic people, just to try different things and see what works for you.

■ **Project yourself.** All the above are about matching the style of the other person, but there is another side to the coin. That is, you want them to enter your world, and do things your way. You might want them to speed up. You might want them to speak more quietly. There comes a time when you want them to do something different. So, after you have responded to someone in their rather loud style, try reducing the volume and hope that their volume will reduce as well.

Join in with other people's 'dances' if you want to communicate with them.

6.8

Share information with those around you

What do we need to achieve when working with difficult people? We need to strengthen relationships, and sharing information is one way to do this. Johari's Window is a tool that helps you identify the level of sharing and blind spots you have.

An example of Johari's Window

	Known to self	Not known to self
Known to others	* Shared information	Blind spot
Not known to others	Private information	Unavailable information

* Open this 'window' for better relationships

case study What needs to be kept private and what can be shared depends to some extent on culture. I once worked with a German who was considered cold, remote and aloof by his fellow managers in the UK. We

The idea behind Johari's Window is that the more you share information with someone, the better your relationship will be. The four squares – or 'windows' – contain different types of information:

■ **Shared information.** This is known to both you and the other party.
■ **Private information.** This is known only to you.
■ **Blind spot.** This is known to the other party, but not known to you.
■ **Unavailable information.** This is not known to either of you.

The idea is to increase the size of the shared information window, so reducing the size of all the other windows. You do this by sharing information that you had previously kept to yourself and encouraging the other party to reciprocate. Any feedback from the other party will increase the shared information and reduce your blind spot at the same time. This way you will almost certainly develop better, more productive relationships at work.

Look on the Internet for different versions of Johari's Window, some of which are interactive. Some require you and at least one other participant to fill in the 'windows' with descriptions of your character, comparing your responses with those of the other participants. The results can be enlightening.

Sharing information does not mean that you have to share intimacies that you wish to keep to yourself. It means sharing ideas with one another on what's important to you: your aspirations and family; likes and dislikes; when you will appreciate help and when you won't.

Share more information to develop more productive relationships.

discussed Johari as a vehicle for improving relationships, and he found his own way of using it to bridge the gap between him and some of his team. Most importantly, the smile count went up!

6.9

Complain effectively

If you are seen as someone who is always complaining, then people will see you as difficult and switch off. Here are a few tips on how to appear reasonable when expressing your concern about something.

In your private life you may complain about poor service, poor workmanship, a lack of standards or inappropriate behaviour. At work you may complain about similar things, but the trick is to make your point without people labelling you a moaner.

The **EEC** feedback tool is very helpful in taking the emotion out of any situation (see also Secret 6.2).

■ **E = give an Example.** "Last week you promised to ring me back and you haven't."
■ **E = explain the Effect.** "This has prevented me from organizing the other building contractors."
■ **C = ask for Change.** "Please keep me updated on progress and ring me when you say you will."

Also consider the points opposite, some of which we have already covered in earlier Secrets.

"Grant me the serenity to accept the things I cannot change, the courage to change what I can, and the wisdom to know the difference"

Reinhold Niebuhr, 20th-century American theologian

Whether you are making a point to colleagues, team members, people in another department, or suppliers:

1 Get your facts right.
2 Talk to someone, rather than send a prickly email.
3 Stick to the point. Don't dilute your case by trying to cover too many issues.
4 Be reasonable, or you will not be listened to and you will be labelled as difficult.
5 Stay calm if you want to avoid the other person becoming difficult. You will achieve much more if you are courteous and polite.
6 Pick the right person. Sometimes it's best to leave it with just one person for them to sort out. On other occasions it may pay you to lobby several people, including senior people. It depends who you want a relationship with.
7 Consider explaining the consequences of it not being dealt with. It's usually best to resort to this when there is no sign of resolution.
8 Be patient. It's linked with being reasonable.
9 Know what you can change and what you can't.

Aim to 'express your concern' rather than 'complain'.

6.10

Use both power and influence

Difficulties arise when any two people have a different impression of what good performance looks like. You need to understand the difference between power and influence if you seek to change things. Who holds the power to change what is happening?

This book is full of examples of the differences, real or imaginary, that cause friction at work. It also has suggestions on behaviour that will allow you to succeed in influencing people. The question of power is something that we have yet to address, and it is important that you recognize where yours comes from. If you have the power of the boss, your strategy might be simply to ask someone to do something. If you don't have that power, your strategy might be to lobby others to achieve your objective.

Look around you for case studies. Who are the people who are most respected and influential? What have they got that makes them successful? Keep observing such people, and learn from them.

one minute wonder List the various things that give you power in your present workplace.

"T'ain't what you do, it's the way that you do it"

From the jazz standard of the same name by Oliver and Young

■ **Power.** This is the capacity that you possess. You may have power because of your position. You may have it because of some special knowledge or expertise. Power comes from your connections and the resources that you can draw upon. Your personal authority and charisma can also be a source of power to you. In any situation, you have to take stock of what power you have, and how much power others have, before deciding your strategy.

■ **Influence.** This is the way that you use what power you have. This book is about both power and influence. It is about giving you power through Secrets; it is also about harnessing whatever power you have, with appropriate behaviour and tools. You will exert influence if you display the behaviours outlined in this book, such as listening, summarizing, managing emotions, being consistent, and taking the trouble to understand those people above you, around you and reporting to you.

■ **Success.** There are 50 bold sentences, one for each Secret, that sum up this book. If you use them, you will successfully use your power to influence those around you and reduce the likelihood of coming up against difficult people.

Before you seek to influence, ask yourself, who has the power?

Resolve conflicts effectively

Our final chapter draws together the key learning points from this book and ensures that your approach to dealing with difficult people will be effective. The checklists help you identify the cause of the situation. The final Secret reminds you to reduce any differences between you and those around you, as well as to reach an accommodation with others on those things that you cannot realistically expect to change.

7.1

Learn together

If you share any learning experience with someone else, you will form a powerful bond with them. But sometimes you will encounter friction because other people learn in different ways to you. The secret is to identify your own learning style and those of the people with whom you are working.

Honey and Mumford (see further reading) developed a questionnaire for identifying preferred learning styles, which can be accessed on the Internet. You could use it under your own initiative in a one-on-one difficult situation, but it is more often used in business as a vehicle for building stronger teams or in a company-wide approach to learning and development. I always use it at the start of any coaching relationship, because it tells me what activities people will readily respond to and what development activities they might struggle with.

Once you have completed the questionnaire, you will have a score for each of four different learning styles. Kolb (see further reading) suggests that we all learn by going through a learning cycle of Doing, Reflecting, Theorizing and Practice. Honey and Mumford suggest that we learn in each of the four styles listed opposite, but that we prefer some more than others.

■ **Activists** learn best by doing things – engaging in activity.
■ **Reflectors** prefer to stand back and think about things.
■ **Theorists** learn best from models, concepts and theories.
■ **Pragmatists** enjoy putting the ideas into practice, fitting them into the workplace.

These ideas will help you best if you:

1 Accept there is no right or wrong in this, just differences that can be a barrier to two people getting on.
2 Understand your own learning style, and use it regularly to play to your strengths.
3 Work on your less-favoured learning style so as to become a more balanced learner. People who are very reflective, for instance, should sometimes stop reflecting and instead plunge themselves into activity.
4 Understand the preferred learning style of your 'difficult' person, and encourage them as they use that style.
5 Encourage your 'difficult' person to develop their less-favoured styles so that they too become a more balanced learner. Activists could be persuaded to stop and reflect.
6 Make learning an experience that you share with those around you. Make the need to learn one of the things that you agree upon, and see how it helps your relationship.
7 Share parts or the whole of your personal development plan with each other. Get personal!
8 Team up to see how the two of you can use your power and influence to change things for both of you.
9 In an increasingly multicultural world, go out of your way to learn about the different cultures around you.

Make learning a shared experience in order to develop good relationships.

7.2

Check your own qualities

Here are some of the key personal qualities needed to develop good relationships. If you check your own capability against this list, or secure feedback from others, you will increase your chances of dealing successfully with difficult people. The tool kit you need contains attitudes, skills and knowledge.

Attitudes you need to cultivate:

- Starting with the end in mind.
- Respecting other people's values, beliefs and opinions.
- Accepting that others won't do it your way.
- Seeking outcomes that are acceptable to all parties.
- Having the courage to accept pressure and face conflict.
- Being flexible. Use 'different strokes for different folks'.
- Being prepared to learn and improve your performance.
- Being open to new ideas.
- Seeking first to understand, then to be understood.
- Accepting that differences will exist.
- Accepting that differences are okay.
- Avoiding unhelpful stereotyping.
- Building trust and/or credibility before seeking to bring about change.
- Being courageous enough to take a measured, calculated risk.
- Accepting responsibility for both successes and mistakes.
- Judging other people's performance, not their character.
- Sharing your knowledge.

Skills you need to demonstrate:

- To step into other people's shoes.
- To listen first, and listen more than you talk.
- To tell it like it is, without spin but with some sensitivity.
- To deliver specific, quality feedback that others will value.
- To stay calm under pressure.
- To display helpful, collaborative body language.
- To set a good example, be a role model and lead.
- To set measures of success, review regularly and reward success.
- To display emotional intelligence.
- To ask questions in order to understand others.
- To be assertive – not submissive and not aggressive.
- To encourage feedback from others.
- To work with positive outcomes and positive language.
- To be straightforward and clear in your communications.
- To visualize success, decide on your strategy and agree a plan of action.
- To deal with people's perceptions as well as with reality.

Body of knowledge you need to build:

- The cultural differences that may be a factor in any specific situation.
- The importance of a psychological contract.
- Recognition of your own beliefs, prejudices, competence and confidence.
- The law, company policy, systems and procedures.
- How to manage third-party and 360-degree feedback.
- How to diagnose the right problem, then how to solve it.
- How to manage emotion when it overrides logic.
- An appreciation of what is changing in the world around you.
- The complete picture that surrounds you and the other person.
- Where the power and influence lie to help you achieve your goals.
- What tools, such as psychometrics, to use in any given situation.
- How to manage change.

Bear in mind that your attitude will drive your behaviour, and that, if you want to, you can change your behaviour more quickly than you can change your attitudes (which are more deep seated).

Check your tool kit of attitudes, skills and knowledge.

7.3

Check the situation

Before you label someone as difficult, work through
this checklist. You may not be in control of all these
factors yourself, so you may need to lobby others to
change some of these things.

There are many difficult situations and factors that prevent
people from giving their best – arguments, redundancies, poor performance, illness, discipline, appraisals, organizational change and vested
interests. All these things may need to be sorted out before your difficult person will be ready to meet your expectations.

1 **Are there any organizational or team issues?** Have there
been any changes in structure or responsibilities?

2 **How much do you and others understand their situation?**
How much do you know of this person and how they go about
their daily work? How reasonable are the demands placed on
them? What systems and procedures are they obliged to follow?
Is someone else causing the problem? Can you understand why
they react as they do?

3 **Are there conflicting departmental interests that are
driving the problem?** Does this person report to others?

4 **Is this person a 'square peg in a round hole' (misfit)?** What motivates them? How valued do they feel? Will they ever be happy and work effectively in this situation?

5 **Have you understood more than just the symptoms of poor behaviour?** Do other people need to spend more time with this person? Have you identified the root cause of this person's behaviour? Is there a lack of leadership? Is there clarity of his or her role? Are there clearly defined expectations?

6 **Are communications sufficiently clear?** Are team briefs in place to give information on progress and what is expected? Is the person involved in the right meetings? Or involved in too many?

7 **Are the right things rewarded?** Are inappropriate things allowed to go unchecked? Is feedback encouraged? Is performance review a way of life?

8 **How helpful is the culture?** Is there mutual respect and trust around the person? Is there a need to accept the value of different styles? Is the culture one that encourages problem-solving, or is it poorly organized chaos?

9 **Who else might be finding this person difficult?** Is their performance acceptable to their team or to the organization?

0 **Will other people share your view?** Is there a need to accept different behaviour because of the positive contribution of the person in question? Will others tolerate the present situation, or will they want to change it?

Take time to understand their situation before you label someone difficult.

7.4

Check if it's the other person

If neither you nor the situation is the problem, you may have a genuinely difficult person on your hands. There is a need to spot this, and to understand why this person is being difficult, before charging into action. This checklist reminds you what to look for.

First let's look at the **symptoms** that you and others might see in your difficult person:

■ **Hostility.** They could be hostile to you, with their spoken and written communications and with their body language.
■ **Lack of interest.** They fail to engage with the people they work with, or lack energy.
■ **Poor performance.** They fail to deliver the results expected of them, or fail to deliver on time.
■ **Low standards.** Their work is sub-standard or erratic, and they ignore requests to improve.
■ **Lack of motivation.** They deliver only the minimum necessary.
■ **Negative outlook.** They see only problems.
■ **Discordant.** They do things differently to everyone else.

"Never attribute to malice or other deliberate decision what can be explained by human frailty, imperfection, or ignorance" Rabbi Harold Kushner

Let's consider some of the many possible **reasons** why people behave like this:

■ **Past experiences.** Experiences of a previous company or culture have affected them badly.

■ **Religious or cultural beliefs.** These might cause them to reject others around them.

■ **Insecurity.** They are fearful for their position, or possibly don't feel valued or trusted.

■ **Unsure of themselves.** They lack confidence in their ability.

■ **You.** They might not like, respect or trust you.

■ **Antipathy.** They dislike their job.

■ **Confusion.** They are unclear about what is expected of them.

■ **Volatility.** They are driven by emotion and ignore logic.

■ **Personal problems.** They may have private issues to deal with.

■ **Grievances.** They may harbour an unspoken sense of unfairness about their role or career.

■ **Lack of support.** They are not getting the help they need.

■ **Personality.** They are unpleasant, devious or selfish, which we can't change much, so it pays not to recruit such people in the first place!

Check the symptoms and root causes before you decide how to approach your problem person.

7.5

Move forward together

If you are having difficulties with any relationship, it is so much easier if you move forward together, and help each other. This secret gathers together some of my favourite ideas from earlier in the book, plus a special look at relationships.

If you expect movement in any relationship to be one way, you are likely to be disappointed. With togetherness in mind, some of our previously considered ideas were:

■ **Learn together.** Link the personal development of yourself and others to the business plan.

■ **Visualize success.** Then turn that into a shared way forward.

■ **Ensure that helping people is part of the culture.** This is easier if it applies to the whole organization, but you can make a dent in this as an individual by supporting and helping those around you.

■ **Agree positive outcomes.** Start with the end in mind – a positive one.

■ **Regularly exchange expectations.** Do this with the key people around you – your boss, colleagues and people in other departments.

"Don't find fault. Find a remedy."

Henry Ford (1863–1947), American industrialist

■ **Check your credibility.** Before you seek to change others, make sure you are credible yourself.
■ **Put first things first.** Demonstrate clearly what your priorities are and how they fit with the priorities of those around you.
■ **Be positive** Use a positive and common language to relate to those you work with.

Now let's summarize the key things that we have covered on relationships.

Relationships that don't work are based on:	Relationships that work are based on:
■ Jealousy	■ Trust
■ Dishonesty	■ Honesty and sincerity
■ Selfishness	■ Openness
■ Arrogance	■ Mutual respect
■ Vested interests	■ Mutual interests
■ A conflict of interest	■ Empathy
■ Indifference	■ Communication

If you want good relationships with those around you, get alongside each other!

7.6

Keep working on the differences

Here are my Top Ten favourite ideas that I would like to leave with you.

1 **Look at the whole picture.** Don't just look at the difficult person. Look at what is going on in the system that is you, the other person and the situation in which you both work.

2 **Close the gap.** Treat difficult relationships as you would treat any problem. Many people use gap analysis as a problem-solving tool. With relationships, there is a need to identify where you are now and where you want to get to. The requirement is to close the gap, so keep asking yourself, "What must I do to close the gap?" Then stick at it!

3 **Trust your instinct.** It's all very well to solve problems, but if your instinct tells you it's wrong, it probably is wrong. Trust your heart.

4 **Tackle it early.** If it feels wrong, tackle it sooner rather than later. Have the courage to act early, because the problem will almost certainly get bigger if you delay. Quiet and early is easier than late and loud.

5 **Help people.** Gain trust by showing that you genuinely want to help them. Be generous with your knowledge. Help people before they ask for it, otherwise they might need more serious help later on.

6 **Think 'win/win'.** Act in such a way that you are perceived as having other people's interests at heart as much as your own. That way you will reduce differences.

7 **Use all resources.** Use all the help that you can lay your hands on. Ask for help from third parties. Consider what tools are available to you, and the best one for any situation.

8 **Try fresh things.** Don't always use the same approach to close gaps. Be creative and use an appropriate method. If the first method doesn't work, try another!

9 **Give it your best shot.** Not all of the difficulties that we have looked at can be sorted out. Sometimes, you need to accept that the situation needs to be totally changed, as in a complete change of job. Sometimes you have to live with what you have. As long as you can go to bed at night with a clear conscience, and say, "I gave it my best shot", you've done your job.

0 **Empathize with others.** Seek first to understand, then to be understood. If you do this, you stand every chance of communicating effectively with those around you.

Think about you and the situation as well as your 'difficult' person, then manage the differences. Good luck!

Jargon buster

360-degree feedback
Feedback from a group of people that work around you – above, below and alongside.

Assertive
It is 'win/win' behaviour; not aggressive, not submissive.

Behaviour
What we do in a specific situation (e.g. shout, listen, confront, appease).

Change curve
A model describing how most people react to change, with tips on how to manage it.

Culture
The way things are done in an organisation or group of people.

Emotional intelligence
The capacity to understand and manage your emotions and the emotions of others.

Empathy
The ability to put yourself in someone else's shoes and see things through their eyes.

Force field analysis
A method of analysis that focuses on the competing forces, for and against, that come into play when making a decision. The positive forces are termed 'helping forces'; the negative factors are termed 'hindering forces'.

Internal customer
The term can be used to refer to a co-worker or separate department within an organization that depends on you or your department for a service in order to complete the overall product or service that the business provides and sells to external customers.

Johari's window
A model for improving relationships.

Kinesthetic
Related to the sense of feeling. In terms of language preference, some people are attuned to words about sound ("let's talk business", "that sounds interesting", etc); some prefer 'visual' words ("I see what you mean", "let's look at the future", etc); while others favour a 'kinesthetic' vocabulary ("I sense you're unsure", "I feel passionate about this", etc).

Measures of success
An alternative way to describe outcomes, objectives, targets and goals.

NLP

Neuro Linguistic Programming (NLP) is a collection of techniques that help people communicate more effectively and overcome performance-limiting behaviours.

Outcomes

What you want to finish up with; the results. Could be called objectives, but outcomes are something that you should be able to visualize.

Personality

The sum of what we are as a result of our genes and our environment (e.g. introvert, extrovert).

Psychological contract

The normally unwritten agreements and promises that exist between you and those round you.

SMART targets

A system for agreeing targets and objectives with those around you, arranged into the acronym SMART. It stands for: Specific, Measurable, Agreed, Realistic and Timed.

Strategy

This is how you plan to achieve your objectives. Usually it is about the big things that you plan to do, but it could also include the things that you plan not to do.

Style

A collective description of the way we do things (e.g. curious, courageous, challenging, etc.).

Timelines

An imaginary line linking past, present and future.

Transactional Analysis (TA)

A tool for developing effective behaviour.

Values

The principles that are important to you and inform your behaviour.

Win Win

A situation in which both parties have reason to feel satisfied with the outcome.

Further reading

Back, Ken and Kate *Assertiveness At Work* (McGraw Hill, 1995) ISBN 978-0077114282

Berne, Eric *Games People Play* (Ballantine Books, 1996, first published 1965) ISBN 978-0345410030

Berne, Eric *What Do You Say After You Say Hello* (Bantam Books, 1974) ASIN: B0011N636A

Borg, James *Persuasion: the Art of Influencing People* (Pearson Education, 2004) ISBN 978-0-2736-8838-9

Bridges, William *Transitions: Making Sense of Life's Changes* (Da Capo Press, 2004, first published 1979) ISBN 073820904X

Covey, Stephen R. *7 Habits of Highly Effective People: Powerful Lessons in Personal Change* (Simon and Schuster, 2004) ISBN 978-0743272452

Denny, Richard *Succeed for Yourself: Unlock Your Potential for Success and Happiness* (Kogan Page 3rd Edition, 2009) ISBN 978-0-7494-5644-3

Dent, Fiona *Working Relationship Pocket Book* (5th Editon, Management Pocketbooks, 2003) ISBN 978 190 377 6971

Goleman Daniel *Working with Emotional Intelligence* (Bloomsbury Publishing, 1999) ISBN 978 074 754 3848

Kotter, John P. and Chen, Dan S. *The Heart of Change: Real-Life Stories of How People Change Their Organisations* (Harvard Business School Press, 2002) ISBN 978 157 851 2546

McCormack Mark H. *What You'll Never Learn on the Internet* (Harper Collins Business 2000) ISBN 978 000 257 1715

Pease, Allan and Barbara The Definitive Book of Body Language: How to Read Others' Attitudes by Their Gestures (Orion 2005) ISBN 978 075 285 8784

Shapiro, Mo *Understanding Neuro-linguistic Programming in a Week* (Hodder & Stoughton, 1998) ISBN 978 034 071 1231

Toropov, Brandon *The Complete Idiot's Guide to Getting Along With Difficult People* (Alpha Books, 1997) ISBN 978 002 861 5974

Reid, Roger H and Merrill, David *Personal Styles and Effective Performance* (CRC Press, 1981) ISBN 978 080 196 8990

Wellin, M. *Managing the Psychological Contract: Using the Personal Deal to Increase Business Performance* (Gower, 2007) ISBN 978 056 608 7264

Norman Leet is contactable by email at norman@evolvetogrow.co.uk

The author's approach to development and performance management is viewable at www.scott-brown.co.uk Details of David Brown's bespoke approach to improving performance can be obtained by emailing David at: davidbrown@scott-brown.co.uk

Useful websites

There is so much material available on the Internet and in archives, and your needs are special to you. You won't want to read all this material, but you can look at the big ideas and search for material to suit your needs. Here are pointers to help you.

Belbin for help with team roles
www.belbin.com

CIPD (Chartered Institute of Personnel & Development) for information about psychological contracts and people management
www.cipd.co.uk

Honey & Mumford for their learning styles questionnaire (LSQ)
www.peterhoney.com

The Work Foundation for effective working
www.theworkfoundation.com

Learning Experience for information about the Kolb learning cycle and other structures
www.learningandteaching.info/learning/experience.htm

Thomas Kilmann for handling conflict
www.kilmann.com

www.BusinessSecrets.net